We Do!
WEDDING VOWS THAT WORK

Compliments of The Barn at Raccoon Creek

We Do:
WEDDING VOWS THAT WORK

(And Keep You Happily Married!)

Rev. Dr. Rob Hundley

ISBN:
ISBN-13: 978-0-9975342-0-7

DEDICATION

I dedicate this book to my wife, Betsy. I would not have written it without your love, dedication, encouragement and insight. Together we are becoming so much more than if we were apart.

CONTENTS

PREFACE

You're getting married - CONGRATULATIONS! Marriage is a big deal and I, for one, am a big fan of it. That is why I have written this book. It can help you if you want to write your own wedding vows. It can also help you make sense out of the traditional vows many couples have used for centuries. Most of all, it will help you think about and gain clarity around the changes and challenges married life offers.

How To Read This Book If You Are Writing Your Vows

Over the years, I have helped hundreds of couples put their weddings together. I have found that couples fall into two categories: those who want to get everything in place several months before the wedding, and those who whip the service together at the last minute.

If you are part of the first group, read this book as you would any other. We will walk through the vow writing process step by step. Before we get to the vows though, we need to look at the overall style of your wedding. What is the frame that surrounds your vows? Far from an afterthought to everything else, your vows are the pinnacle of your wedding. Knowing how the rest of the pieces fit together gives you a great starting point.

You get to work on your actual vows in Chapter 2. When I meet with couples, one of my favorite ties is sitting back after asking how they met. That answer can be kind of awkward for some. But every couple lights up when I ask next, "When did you know that it was real love?" Start your vows off at this very personal place. Everyone can relate to it and it will forever ground your vows in your memory.

It is easiest to look at marriage from three broad perspectives: Love, Livelihood, and Legacy. Chapters 3–5 bring your focus to each of these areas. Each one becomes a conversation starter for the two of you. Set aside a time to talk about your answers with your fiancé. As you go along you will find that there may be some issues you haven't thought all the way through. You may find that there are some assumptions and expectations that they will need to clarify and not take for granted. Most couples find that they have much more areas of agreement and the process is very empowering.

Talking on this level is a great habit to get into. Plan ahead. Remove distractions. Devote your full attention. Doing this now will set the stage for all future big discussions. You will come away with a clearer picture of your lives together. Your vows are how you will describe that picture to each other.

As long as we are being clear about things, what are your deal breakers? Everybody has them, but few want to discuss them out in the open. Chapter 6 gives you a framework for the hard, but oh so important work of setting boundaries.

You are in the homestretch now. From here you will pull your thoughts together around your vows, polish them up and put on the finishing touches. Chapter 7 provides some ideas on how to go about all of this. Once you get to this point, you can either do this together or separate, it is up to you. However you go about the process, let this be a jumping off point to strengthen your marriage and get it off on the right foot.

As for you last minute-ers, for now, let's just call you, oh, I don't know, 'Grooms.' Have no fear. I have you covered here too. Flip to the homework sections behind Chapters 2–6. Fill those out and then flip to the Putting It All Together section behind Chapter 7. I figure you can write a pretty good draft of your vows in under thirty minutes.

If you are one of these procrastinator, put your right hand up and repeat after me, "I, state your name, do solemnly swear that I will read the supporting chapters within three months from today." If your spouse suspects that you had this book for all this time and did nothing until the last minute, read the section in Chapter 6 about honesty before responding. Once you have fulfilled your pledge to read the rest of the book, find some time and talk about your strengths and challenges as a couple.

How This Book Will Help If You Are Using Traditional Vows

Then there are those of you who will be using a traditional version of marriage vows. This book can still be very helpful to you too. Having an idea of what the words mean that you are repeating back after your wedding officiant is vital to laying a solid foundation for your marriage.

You might think that you can pass over the homework sections. But why not use these exercises as a way to really deepen your bond?

Once you have read this book and filled in the blanks, share your thoughts with your spouse or spouse-to-be. It will be easy to see the points where you agree and the points that will need more time and energy.

Hey, here's an idea. Why not take the time to write a set of vows yourselves? You don't have to use them during your ceremony. Write your own personal vows. Find a romantic moment and say them to each other out loud. Trust me, it will be a good thing. Both for the vows you are writing as well as the corresponding areas of your relationship.

Regardless of whether you write your vows for your wedding or for another time, DO NOT, I repeat, DO NOT under any circumstances, put your wedding vows that you have just worked so hard on, in a box to be forgotten in a closet! Find a way to remind yourselves of them on a regular basis. Print them, frame them and hang them somewhere where you will see them every day. Show them to your families. Explain them to your children. Trot them out on your anniversaries. May they become your most treasured possession. Just like your marriage.

As my gift to you, I have taken the vow writing worksheets and put them on my web site. To download them, please go to: www.FrameYourVows.com/gift

Can I Read This Book If I Am Already Married?

Nope. I am sorry. You're stuck. OF COURSE YOU CAN READ IT! In many ways you are in the best place of all. As you read along, remember your own wedding day. So few people actually do remember it. Use your photos and videos as prompts. Think too of the challenges you two have faced along the way. You know much of the material here because you have lived it. At the time, you might not have agreed, but that is a good thing. Use this as an opportunity to rededicate yourselves to each other. Write a set of vows, share and celebrate them in a way that is special for you.

INTRODUCTION

I am not so naive as to suggest that simply by following the advice in this book to better understand your wedding vows, you will live with your spouse happily ever after. But if it were true, wouldn't you do it? Of course you would. Getting married is one of the greatest decisions you ever make. It can also be one of the scariest. I have stood beside hundreds of couples at the lovers' leap precipice saying, "On your mark, get set, jump!" Will you spread your wings and soar off into the blue skies together, or will you tumble to the rocks below?

Maybe that is painting marriage in a rather stark light. Let's back up and not get ahead of ourselves. No doubt you received all sorts of reactions when you told people you were tying the knot. Mothers cry. Friends scream and hug you. Other friends look like they want to say something, but think better of it. Still, other friends may pull you aside and ask if you are sure. One thing is true for all of these reactions. Marriage is a big step and the emotional energy is strong.

Getting married is something that takes a lot of thought and intention. It is not something that you can quickly or easily take a 'do over.'

Really, my lovers' leap image is about the importance of planning for your marriage. With that said, let's go back to the image.

Standing as you are now, waiting your turn to jump, you hold a scrap of paper with some words on it in your hand – your vows. They are not some nonsense phrase to shout into the wind. Rather, they are sound words of guidance. Your vows are what your marriage is all about. Traditional vows have been polished over the centuries. Self-written vows hold a personal dedication. Both are very powerful, and, if you heed them, will lift you two high into the sky.

But who ever takes the time to understand their vows when they are standing at one of the pinnacles of their life? The traditional words are old and confusing. If you wrote your own vows, did you cover everything? It's too much to think about on your wedding day. Let's just get on with the rest of the ceremony, and get to the reception.

Funny thing, because as it turns out, it was during just this time between ceremony and reception that the idea for this book came to me. The father of the groom had just approached me. He shook my hand, thanked me for the service, and then pulled me in close. "Do they have any idea what they are getting themselves into?"

Do you? Do any of us? The simple answer is no, none of us knows what we are getting into when we say "I do." Some days, being married is the most wonderful, incredible, fantastic experience that could possibly be. Other times, it can be painful. The vast majority of days are somewhere in between.

Too often, we don't know if it is a good day or a bad day until it is too late. So we think that they just randomly occur. We think we either had too little or too big a hand in creating the great days. And on the bad ones, well, we just have no idea when things went so wrong.

If only there was some way for us to plan for and even maximize the number of great days that we have together. And what if we could head off, or at least minimize, the bad? Is there some way that we could just get off on the right foot?

Wait, what's that in your hand? Why it's your vows, the words you used to start this off in the first place. I believe that's where the answer lies. The words themselves are not magical. Yet they do hold great power. All words spoken from the heart do.

In my career, I have been honored to say to hundreds of couples, "Repeat after me..." We have said vows in hallowed churches, mountain meadows, living rooms, backyards – even beside the bar of a '19th hole' after the ceremony was rained out on at the golf course. I have also sat with many other couples in my office as they cried through tissue after tissue trying to figure out why they are having such a hard time relating to each other. While I much prefer to be with a couple in the former rather than later position, I realize that my role in both is very similar. How do I help them keep their love alive? The ones with a real shot are those who are fully invested. If you start off today, fully committed to your marriage, your vows will guide you all your days together.

The key is speaking them from your heart. Even if you don't change one word of the traditional wedding vows, after reading this book you and your partner will have a much better understanding of what you are agreeing to.

And if you do write your own wedding vows, this book will guide you step-by-step through the process. Having a better understanding of your vows gives you a better start and greater potential for success in your marriage.

More than anything, this book was written to support your intentions behind the vow and covenant you are making. I haven't met anyone who wanted their marriage to fail. Most couples probably know that you need to be committed to working at making it work. The challenge is that many of us do not know where to focus our attention. It is as if we all somehow think that you just know how to be married through osmosis. It just happens when you say the magic words. Again, there are no magic words that will ensure you stay happily married. There are, however magic intentions. If you and your partner are deeply committed to your marriage, there is a very good chance that it will succeed. Dedicate yourselves to writing and, or, understanding your vows and you are starting off on the right foot.

Being fully invested in your vows does several things. It makes the vision of your marriage explicit. Neither of you gets to say, "I didn't sign on for this,"... whatever this might be. You have taken the time to look at and consider the 'this' and 'thats.'

There is also something powerful about the process itself. These are not always light and fun conversations. You have to consider some of the hard stuff that marriage includes. Commend yourselves for the maturity to do that.

Finally, this lays the groundwork for the very powerful habit I spoke of before - talking. It is in this sharing that we truly grow to become greater than the sum of our parts.

Chapter 1

Dearly Beloved

Imagine standing where I do at weddings. The groom and his groomsmen have come forward and we are all watching the bridesmaids walk down the aisle. Let your gaze drift across the guests.

We see a young couple slip into a couple of seats in the back row. You recognize her as a friend from work. Him, let's call him 'plus 1,' and he looks pretty nervous. You remember when you two were them. Going to a wedding together can be a big step in early dating. What sort of public statement are we making? Is he or she going to make an assumption about where we are headed? Am I going to catch 'it'?

There are a few more couples we need to meet. Several rows closer to the front is a couple who are friends of your parents. He is on his phone, checking the score of the game. She is watching the bridesmaids. She looks back at her husband and you can see a frown pass over her face. They are not sitting close and by their body language look even farther apart. They do not look like the couple you want to become.

Up close to the front is an elderly woman sitting alone, but she is still a couple. She is your grandmother. This is the first major family function since your grandfather passed. You can see her eyes are glistening with sadness. But you can also feel the sense of love and joy that she has for you on your special day. In that moment, you know what bittersweet looks like.

The music changes and everyone stands up. It is hard to see through them, and then there is the bride, standing at the end of the aisle. Your eyes meet and so do your souls.

There are so many emotions welling up inside. You know that this is the right thing, but it is such a big thing. People mess this big thing up on a regular basis. How do you stop from making those mistakes? You know that it takes hard work. You know that each of you is the right one - the one who makes the hard work worthwhile.

In four quick images you see the wide range of relationships. New and freshly starting out, it is a matter of trying to figure it all out. Am I ready to commit to a marriage? Is this one 'The One'? You are mature enough to know that happily ever after doesn't just happily happen on its own. Too often, couples drift apart, each living in silence and shadow.

Neither wants to admit there is a problem. We avoid change until we can't avoid it anymore and often by then it is too late. But you also see the power of love in an old woman's face. Could it be that love lasts beyond death? Finally, there is your soon-to-be spouse. Of all of these images, this is the most important because it involves you. How you start and work at your marriage will say a lot about where it will ultimately take you.

Step back and ask yourself, "How did we get here?" Marriage is a foundational element found in nearly every society and culture. Its roots are both in civilization and religions. It may seem odd to our way of thinking, but love came relatively late in the tradition. Historians suggest that love only factored into marriage beginning in the twelfth century.

Prior to that, marriages were a way to solidify political and financial power. It was the way to establish who were legitimate heirs. In this sense, marriage is a stabilizing force in society. Many cultures arrange marriages with this goal in mind. It plays a role, albeit a relatively cold and impersonal one.

Today, it is love, of course, that is the primary factor for marriage in western culture. Love adds strength to the stability of monogamy and marriage. And with it comes fire and passion, that emotional energy we spoke of before.

At some point, depending on who you listen to, we also mixed religion into the equation. Some say that it goes all the way back to the Jewish creation story of Adam and Eve. God establishes and sanctifies marriage way back then. Others will tell you that the church did not get involved with marriage much before the eleventh century. Soon after, the catholic church established that marriage was a sacrament that the church bestowed on worthy couples.

Other denominations see marriage as a covenant, or a contract made between the couple and God. Still others see God as the giver of the true love shared by the couple and that a marriage is celebrated in recognition and thanksgiving for this gift of love.

Be it civil or religious, authorities have established rules concerning who could marry based on economic status, race, and age. Today we are witness to another significant shift in the evolution of marriage. Keeping the elements of strength and stability in the midst of these changes is vital. Just as marriage will continue to grow and evolve, it will continue to be a bedrock foundation for us.

With this as a starting point, let's look at how all of this goes into making a wedding.

For my first twenty-five years of performing wedding ceremonies, I did them in my capacity as an ordained minister. I conducted weddings for members of my congregation as well as folks who wanted to get married in the big white church in the center of our New England town. I also performed a lot of weddings outside the church. These were done everywhere from homes and backyards to country club golf courses and event centers. I even did one in the 19th hole bar and grill when one of those golf course weddings got rained out. Today I perform weddings throughout the Rocky Mountain region. This has taken me to mountain meadows and beside rushing creeks.

One of the first things that I have noticed about performing weddings in these various settings is that the setting itself goes a long way toward setting the tone and the mood. Chances are you have already established how your wedding will feel. You may well have chosen your venue based on this feel. This will also help to shape the form of vows that you will use.

When I meet with a couple to plan their service and help them with their vows, I use the following grid:

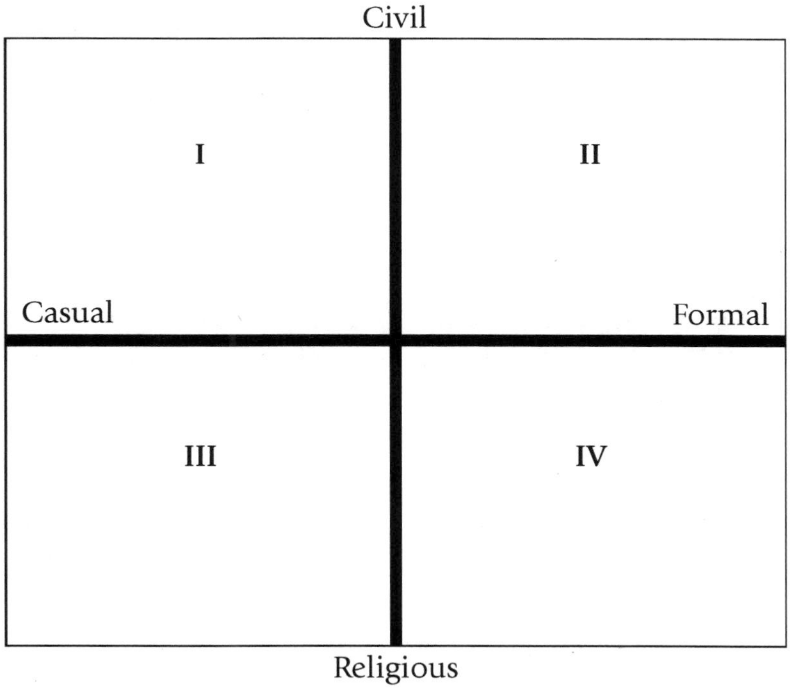

A wedding in Quadrant I might well be one of those I have performed beside a mountain stream. The setting and the attire set a more relaxed mood. The elements of the ceremony are not religious, but intentional nonetheless. A Quadrant II service might be at an Event Center or Banquet Facility. These are more formal in style and also without religious tones. When more religious aspects like prayers and clergy are added, we move into a Quadrant III or IV style of service. These could certainly be conducted in a church or religious setting, but they don't have to. It has more to do with recognizing what elements and aspects are relevant and meaningful to you.

The style of wedding you have has a connection with your vows. Ceremonies that are more formal are better suited for more traditionally framed vows. These vows include such phrases as 'love, honor and cherish,' 'in sickness and in health,' and 'till death do us part.' In a few chapters we will start to unpack these phrases for their deeper meanings. While you can certainly use the traditional words, you might also reword them, keeping in mind your overall style of service. A more formal style would mean that the language might be more serious. Vowing to be your partner's 'snuggle bunny for life' could seem very out of place.

Some say formal is passé. I think that it depends entirely on the couple. Many folks place a greater sense of importance on the occasion with a more formal approach. I once had a couple who were very relaxed and casual, even by Colorado standards. They really surprised me when they both said that they wanted a very formal service. The bride replied, "We may be laid back and all, but our love is the single greatest thing in the world." "I give respect where I think respect is due. So let's do this thing formal," said the groom.

I think that the abrupt change in their style spoke volumes to their families and guests about just how invested the two of them were.

Casual styles allow for more freedom when it comes to vows. That can be a good thing, or a not so good thing. It means that you need to spend significant time working on your vows, lest the casual style implies a lack of commitment. "I'm cool with you chillin' at my crib playing Xbox" may mean the same as," All that I have is yours." But each suggests different levels of investment in the relationship.

Several years ago I had a couple who vowed to 'burn their knees' for each other. Turns out the groom had burned his knee on very hot pavement while proposing. In their casual setting, this phrase fit perfectly.

The decision to go more casual or more formal may be easy compared to the next choice. Do you want to include religion, or is yours a civil or legal service?

Coming from a religious background, I think that couples assume I am pushing my faith on them. When I tell them that the service is much more about the two of them than it is me, I think they often think that I am using some reverse psychology and that I really do wish they would go the religious route.

Personally, I believe that love is the greatest gift with which God has blessed us. Love is the greatest force in the universe. When you are lucky enough to find it with another person, I think it is a tremendous gift. Giving thanks for that gift and even asking for help to keep it going strong are very comfortable and natural feelings for me.

Not everyone shares this opinion. You may feel that your religious tradition puts too many demands or attaches too many strings. Maybe you have even been hurt or abused by others in God's name and it is too hard to separate that from your understanding of God. I respect where you are coming from.

Your commitment and dedication to each other is just as strong whether you decide on a more civil or religious ceremony. Your sincerity is what counts. Find the expression that best reflects the two of you.

Some faiths consider the vows that are made to be holy and sacred. Nevertheless, religions place a great amount of emphasis on marriage and the forms weddings can take.

While marriage is described in both the Hebrew and Christian Testaments, there are no specific instructions or even vows for a wedding found in the Bible.

As such, depending on their tradition, priest, ministers, rabbis and other religious men and women may have to follow their services word for word. They may require that you use their set of vows for the service. If that is the case, I believe there is a way if you still want to write your own vows to do so.

You may have to wait until after the wedding ceremony and for all the activity to die down. But while everything is still very fresh, work through the exercises in this book and write your own vows. Once you have them ready, find a time and a place and make them special as you say them to each other. They do not need to compete with the vows you said during your wedding. Instead they can add to and affirm those vows in your own words.

Vows are not something we commonly say. They are a pledge or an oath. Wedding vows are in the same category of importance as a president or elected government official vowing to preserve, protect and defend the ideals of their country. It is as serious as a soldier pledging to serve in an armed force. They are serious, important, and for real.

Vows are spoken too, in public for all to hear and remember. There is a power in saying something that goes deeper than just writing can convey. Part of that might be the intention and the personal manner of speaking. No one can confuse that it was you who said these words.

I think this medium of speech adds to the power of the message it conveys. There is power in hearing your partner say their vows to you. Saying your vows to each other can be one of the most intimate and powerful moments you will share as a couple. My standing joke at the rehearsal is that my wife doesn't like it when other people marry me, so please look at each other when you say your vows. Then, at the wedding, I like to slow the pace down so that the couple really puts intention behind their words. It can be dangerous when you are dealing with such powerful emotions, but luckily I have not had a couple explode yet.

It is sobering and affirming to hear the words as they come out of your own mouth, too. Integrity is the key. We value character qualities like honesty, integrity, commitment and truth. Speaking your vows speaks to your character. Can you be counted on? Are you honest? Are you going to stay and see things through to the end? We all like to think our answers to these questions is a resounding YES. Often it is only in hindsight that we get the chance to see what we are really made of. It is also in these experiences where we can grow in our strength of character.

Elvis impersonators aside, who you say your vows in front of matters as well. Priests, ministers, rabbis, judges, officiants all carry a certain level of respect. The same can be said about parents, family members and friends. More than just an excuse for a great party, bringing everyone who is important to you together can really add to the power of your vows. I am a big fan of those traditions that ask all of the guests to sign the wedding license as witnesses. I have often asked all of the guests to say, "We do!" after I have asked if they promise their support to the vow s you two are making to each other. That can be a pretty important thing for a couple to hear.

All of this is to say that vows are serious and important. They are not meant to be taken lightly or without thought. But then, you wouldn't be reading this book if those things applied to you.

Lastly, vows have a general scope to them bigger than day to day life. You vow to love and honor each other. While taking out the garbage or replacing the toilet paper roll may fit into that, they usually are not mentioned in a vow. We will spend much more time looking at what goes into a set of vows in the coming chapters.

Chapter 2

What Have We Gotten Ourselves Into?

I had worked with Austin and Randi (not their real names, I do not break confidence.) for several months. They were very committed to their relationship. As we met to plan the service, they asked if I could provide them with pre-marital counseling. Over the course of our meetings it was clear that they had put a lot of time and effort into their decision.

We were meeting the week before their wedding to tie up any loose ends and to put the finishing touches on their service. I was shocked when Austin said that he was getting cold feet. Randi was dismayed.

I smiled at Austin, trying to assess the situation and buy some time, not sure what to make of his statement. I dared not look at Randi, but you could feel her tension. He went on, "I don't have cold feet about Randi or how I feel about her. But this is a big step. How can I be sure that I am doing the right thing?"

It suddenly hit me. He was taking all of this very seriously. Now, I don't want to stereotype, but in my experience, if one of the couple is going to be less serious about getting married, it is going to be the groom.

It wasn't his choice in a bride that he was questioning. Rather, it was the importance of the step itself. As the three of us talked, it became clear to Randi that rather than a bad thing, Austin's comment was actually a very deep, profound and good thing.

When I meet with couples, one of my favorite questions is to ask what attracted the two of you to each other? And then from that, how did you know that getting married was in the cards?

I have gotten some very strong answers. I have also had some couples look at me with hesitancy and fear as if thinking, 'How does anyone ever really know?' "How can I be sure that getting married is the right thing?"

If you haven't asked yourself that question by now, it may be important to ask yourself now. Starting at the beginning, there was some sort of attraction that you felt to your fiancé. It may well have been a whole set of attributes they possess.

Take a moment and remind yourself of them. Was it how they look at life? How about their balance of work and play? Was it their sense of humor? What drew you to them physically? As your relationship developed, how have you come to trust and confide in them?

- How do you know that they will have your back?
- What did you learn about them after your first argument?
- How did they connect and fit into the other areas of your life?
- Are there strengths in their family that you admire?

This isn't a decision just for the moment, or even this season of your life. How do you see your lives playing out from generation to generation? What qualities do you see in them that leads you to think that they will be a great parent and even grandparent with you? What about them is it that suggests that you want to spend your life with them.

Comedian Aziz Ansari puts this in very stark terms. It goes something like this: "I like hanging out with you and all. Let's keep doing it until one of us dies!"

And yet, you know it when you know it. This person is the one. You really do believe and feel with all of your heart that they are who you are going to live with and love for the rest of your life.

Different father, but the same question as before. Actually it is one of the more common questions I get at weddings. I had finished up a wedding. The happy couple, their bridal party and the guests' attention was down at the end of the aisle. I started to make my way back too when the father of the bride stuck out his hand. I shook it and he drew me in close." Padre, do you think that they even have a clue of what they have just done?"

"Probably not," I replied, "I sure didn't."

"Me neither, and yet look at me now, twenty-seven years. Sure it hasn't been easy. But I have grown and become someone much better for it. Every morning I give thanks for our love and for our hard work."

Marriage takes a lot of both love and hard work. I think that we often think of these two as some sort of yin and yang. It is as if we have to trade one for the other. I don't think that is necessarily the best way to look at these two.

Rather each adds to or opens the door for the other. I think this father got it right in saying that he was thankful for both.

As we start to focus on your vows, I invite you to think of your love and this challenging work as supportive of each other. My guess is that by answering the following questions about yourselves and each other you are going to find your love growing and your bond strengthening. Ready?

This first set of questions probably fit better into a pre-engagement time. They focus on things that would help you make your decision to get engaged. If you didn't think about these specific things before you got engaged, you probably thought about them on some deeper or intuitive level. You just knew it was the right step.

These questions are designed to help you get it out of your mind and onto paper. They can be answered alone or together. Answering them by yourself might be a good idea for more couples. It can be hard to open up like this unless you have had some practice. The important thing is to be as honest as you can. Generally there are no right or wrong answers, just your answers.

When you feel good about your answers, find a comfortable way to share them. It may be hard not to, but let each other speak without contradicting or objecting. Instead, be open to the other's point of view. I hope that this goes without saying, but remember this is a very intimate and revealing conversation. Take it seriously. Don't laugh or put each other down. The trust that you build your relationship on comes from times like this.

If you choose to work on these together, watch out that you do not answer for each other. Chances are, one of the reasons you were attracted to each other was that they saw things in you that you didn't see in yourself. That is great. But here we are more interested in how you see yourself and then how you see your relationship from your side of it.

Set?

SPOILER ALERT! Your spouse to be did not grow up with the same assumptions, expectations, values and beliefs that you did. These things are the basis on which your answers lie. This difference is a good thing. It gives your relationship a broader foundation. Listen - you will learn from each other.

The strength of your relationship doesn't lie in how similar your answers are to each other. It lies in your ability to identify and then navigate through the differences.

Go!

Start with the each of you, individually.

- What are your own positive gifts and qualities?
- What do you like about you?
- What are your strengths?
- What are the things that you will not compromise on?
- How have you learned and grown over your life so far?

Now move on to the two of you together.

- How do you mesh together?
- How do his/her strengths play into yours?

- Which of you two is better equipped at which decisions and choices?
- In what areas do you both lack enough that it would be wise to seek outside help?
- Where do you see you two clashing?
- How will you work to recognize and defuse these situations before they lead to arguments and anger?

I hope that wasn't too scary. This is all important stuff that can really help out in the years to come. This is where marriage can make you into deeper and better people. When we talk about marriage being hard work, this is what we mean. Every couple I have ever talked with, professionally or just casually, has said the same thing. The more you know the answers to these questions, the smoother your relationship goes. It is when you forget them that trouble and discord can creep in.

Knowing yourselves will help tremendously when you find yourselves tried and tested. It may be hard work, but it is good work and you can do it. Hard work opens the door into deeper levels of love and commitment. Deeper love allows for greater trust. As the years go by and your marriage goes through transformations, it will be good to come back to this.

Remember back in the 'twitterpated' time, you may barely have the thought to ask, much less answer these questions. It may have been all one big, glorious blur. This stuff wasn't even on our radar. "You are the moon to my sun. Who cares if we are so very different? I feel so alive. This is super awesome!" That is all the thought many have put in at that point. Everything is emotion and afire.

But then, things start to grow after you come up for air. The more you get to know, the more you like. You let each other into deeper and more intimate parts of yourselves. 'Twitterpation' gives way to something deep and awesome. And then it happens. One of you blurts out the 'L' word. To the surprise of the two of you, the other responds, "I love you too." It may be time to change your Facebook status.

Perhaps you have become that couple we saw in the back of the wedding, your friend and their 'plus 1'. What were those questions again? Now they start to seem more important.

You go through a cycle or two of life. You have your first big argument. You survive it. You meet each other's families and friends. You become comfortable and familiar with each other. You anticipate and make allowances for each other. You are committed, and now the questions move to a whole new level of meaning and importance. The challenge though is that the further you go, the more assumed the answers become.

Besides, there is still all this wonderful love to wrap up in like a blanket of kittens. Who wants to ask stupid old questions that might make us think? Not me! Let's sleep away the afternoon safe in each other's arms.

I get it. Everything lines up against working through these challenging questions. But they are still important. I realize there is very little about this that sounds romantic. It sounds like we are buying a new car. I am just advocating that we give at least the same amount of rational thought to getting married that we do to buying a car. Excuse the snarky, sarcastic comment, but I hope that I get you thinking in addition to loving.

This brings us back to Austin. He loves Randi. That wasn't the question in his mind when he confessed his cold feet. Of course it was the first thing to come to her mind.

No, his question was how did he **know** that this was the right time? Had he gone through all the steps? He didn't want to somehow get it wrong. Austin wanted assurances. I don't blame him. Marriage is a huge step. We don't want to mess it up. How can we be sure?

I am afraid that I have to give you the same answer I gave him. "I don't know that you ever really know that you know." That is the leap part. This is where faith and trust come into play too.

Perhaps you have been right where Austin was. What began in a naive haze of emotions has given way to harder and deeper looks and questions. Doubts rise up, are addressed and resolved. Questions lead to other questions. Patterns, habits and expectations all grow with our time and experiences together. You go deeper and deeper until one day you realize that you know as much as you are going to that he or she is 'The One.' And now that you have asked all the questions you can think to ask, it is back to following your heart. "Will you marry me?"

"YES!" We get back up from our collective knee. We call our family and friends. We start planning the wedding. We chose our colors and our caterer.

Now that we have made our choice, can we put these questions away? Many do. They put them away for good. We have put in all the thought we are going to. Remember that couple at the wedding, the husband checking the score and the shadow on the wife's face? How do you think they got to where they are now? It sure wasn't exactly intentional. By not intending to work on their marriage, they have let it fall into disrepair. If they continue on, it will likely lead to ruin.

Now, before you get married, is the perfect time to set up some healthy habits for you two to follow for the rest of your lives.

One of the healthiest things you can do as a couple is communicate. When it comes to communication, at least one of you is probably pretty good with the talking part. Expressing yourself is great: this is what I like; this is what I don't; I think that we should do so and so. But there is so much more to communication than just talking.

Listening is huge. I joke that I can repeat the last twenty-seven words that my wife has said. Of course that is not really listening. Listening is creating and holding a space in which your partner feels safe and comfortable telling you deeper and deeper thoughts, hopes, dreams, and fears.

The first step in this is build trust. Trust takes time. As you get to know someone, you come to trust them with deeper, more personal thoughts. Trust gets tested. You prove yourself as trustworthy as you hold, appreciate and respect these things.

We are broken and battered by life. We look for another to provide a little peace and solace.

This is especially true when it comes to fears and self-doubts. Someone to tell us that we are worthy and of great value.

From this secure place you can also share your hopes and dreams. Your spouse will be one of your greatest champions, always in your corner, supporting and encouraging you. The better you two can communicate, the stronger your security and support will be.

Working on this as a couple takes time and practice. It is the foundation upon which you now stand. Or it could be. Take the time to be intentional about building it. As you work on your vows, together, or even apart, it will be good to explore these deeper issues.

You may have noticed that this sounds an awful lot like pre-marital counseling. Isn't this supposed to be a book about wedding vows? Yes, it is, and it is also more. I would argue that they are both very closely related. In some ways your vows are letters that you are writing to yourselves in the future.

The first step in writing vows is deciding what is important enough to include. There will probably be a lot of overlap between the two of you as to what is important. That is good. But equally good and even harder to recognize is being able to honor what your partner sees as important regardless of how you feel about it. We want to make sure that we have all the content that matters. These were the things that were important to you back here. The next couple of chapters are designed to help you get these issues out on the table. Once you know what you want to include in your vows, then you can write and polish them.

While your future experiences as a married couple will shape some of these things that are important to you, the content of your wedding vows will guide you more. It is good to at least have some of the big parts identified. That way your vows can guide you two together in the years to come. When you face a big decision in the years ahead, look at what you have written. Your vows will always be there to remind and guide you.

In my experience, very few couples ever get this explicit about the issues that are important to them. They just go on assumptions and expect that their views are shared by their mate. I was talking with a couple about this not long ago. They are both successful business people. They told me that they were the only couple that they knew who talked about this before they got married. Both of them had been married before and wanted to 'get it right' this time. They actually sat down and wrote out a mission statement for their marriage. That may be overkill. But it speaks to the importance they place on their vows. When I look at them, I see a very strong couple.

Now before you write this off as the most un-romantic idea you have ever heard, the bride confided that they each used some pretty unorthodox bargaining and negotiating tactics. "I am pretty sure no one would consider them to be standard business practices.", she said with a twinkle in her eye.

So go back over the questions again. Better, find someone who can help you two through them or ones like them. Invest a little time, energy and yes, even money into the process. These conversations lift up the content. When you feel that you have done a pretty good job with the pre-engagement questions, take a crack at this first vow writing exercise. This exercise will help you get some of the opening lines out on paper, so that you can start out with some substance. Later on you will shape and polish these ideas into beautiful vows.

Vow Writing Exercise #1

Introductory Words

1. What is one of the best things about your partner?

____

____

____

2. How do their strengths compliment yours?

____

____

____

3. When did you know that they were 'The One'?

____

____

____

4. What silly little thing have you learned to love?

____

____

____

The next three chapters will divide your vows into three broad categories: love, livelihood and longevity. If those don't all make sense now, don't worry. They will. I have broken the traditional vows into these three broad groups. The subtitle of each chapter contains the section of the traditional vows to which it relates.

If you are using traditional vows, I hope that this gives you a deeper sense of their meaning. If you are writing your own, they are a pretty good jumping off point.

Chapter 3

A Promise To Love

"I vow to love you from this day forth,
forsaking all others"

The air was electric. It was the early years of same sex weddings. I was attending the service of two very good friends. Everyone was abuzz about being there. It had a distinctly conspiratorial feel, even for the liberal setting of Boulder, Colorado.

I was curious how the officiant would handle the political and cultural overtones. My curiosity was resolved by his opening words. "Beloved of God, we are here for one reason, and one reason only Love."

With those words, he framed what became a beautiful service. What had the potential of becoming a defiant shot across the bow of society turned on those words into the focus of every other wedding: love.

Aaahhhh, love. The deepest, most profound of human emotions. I believe that we are closest to our divine purpose and calling when we love. I see the love that we feel for another as a God given gift. Lord knows I have done precious little to deserve the vast amount of love that I feel from my wife. As for the love I feel for her, well,

I don't know how I could **not** love her. It is simply and undeniably there.

I often use two scripture verses when speaking of love at weddings. The first one is Paul's words in 1 Corinthians about the quality of love. It is patient and kind. It doesn't insist on its own way and it rejoices in the right.

The second passage comes from the lesser known Song of Solomon. It ends with this, "Many waters cannot quench love, Nor will rivers overflow it; If a man were to give all the riches of his house for love, they would be utterly despised."

I guess you could say that I think of love as a force or power. It may sound odd, but it was not all that long ago that this force was not assumed when two people came together to be married. Just a few hundred years ago, marriage had much more to do with business or politics than romance or love. Royal families married their children to each other to create and strengthen alliances between their countries.

Beyond politics, people married to create business partnerships. The son of a merchant would marry the banker's daughter to ensure favorable lending terms. Others who marry at or above their 'station in life' were viewed as wise. Marrying another with no thought as to financial gain or security was seen as folly. At the very least, marriage offered the potential of having children who would then be legal heirs, able to carry on the family farm or business and provide their parents with security and income in retirement. Marriage was the way this legacy was tracked.

That was then. This is now. In western cultures today, love is the first and foremost factor in deciding to get married. While finances and children factor into marriage and wedding vows, they take a back seat to love.

Jamie was the daughter of one of my church members. She lived out of town and wanted to get married in our church. I sat down with her and her fiancé, Michael, for the first time when they had come back to visit over the holidays.

Jamie pulled a notebook out and started to take very thorough and detailed notes of everything I was saying. I have to admit that my ego was getting pretty puffed up as she hung on my every word, practically writing them down verbatim. She asked my thoughts on love and as I shared them, she wrote with even more enthusiasm. As she wrote she opined, "Oh, that's good. That is a great definition. I am going to have to remember that point."

I began to feel my ego deflate, replaced with something more akin to anxiety and concern. "Umm, I don't mean to be rude, but you two are getting married because you love each other, right?" It was beginning to feel like I was being interviewed by a robot or alien who had never felt love for themselves.

"Oh, God yes! I am writing this down for the conversation I am anticipating having over Christmas dinner. I come from a long line of engineers and scientists. As a poet, I am always at a loss to communicate with them about feelings."

Michael chimed in, "As a musician I am not much help. When we announced our engagement, I thought

I was going to get grilled about how can the two of you make enough to survive?"

"My father was much more concerned with asking us how we knew we are right for each other?" noted Jamie. "When I told him that we loved each other, he said, 'You are going to have to explain that to me sometime."

Indeed, if love is a power, maybe even something of a living thing, then how does it grow between two people? As you come to trust and reveal yourself to another, love begins to stir in your heart. Or maybe you feel love first and trust in that emotion as you start to open up. Either way, a connection forms that draws you deeper into the other. They become your first thought in the morning and your last thought at night. They become the reason that pushes you beyond yourself to be your best. In time, their needs become at least equal to if not greater than your own.

I started out my ministerial career working with a great old country minister. I asked him one day while we were bumping along a dirt road in his beat up pick-up truck how he did pre-marital counseling. He laughed and said that he didn't do much. "I really just have one question, 'Do you love them?' And then when they look at me a little offended and emphatically say 'Yes!', I ask them, 'Well then, would you die for them?' I hold their gaze and in that moment I get a pretty good idea of how ready they are for the plunge they are about to take."

All these years later, and I still think that is a pretty good counseling style. Of course you can run into people who have a low sense of themselves and would sacrifice themselves for just about anyone. But even there, the point of the question finds its mark. Love is love, a most powerful force that defies logic or explanation.

Ask yourself this question: would you give up all that you have, your very life for your intended?' Why? Why not? I actually think this is not meant to be a hypothetical question, either. If love is truly unconditional, you can't include conditions in your answer like, "Well, if it was fifty years from now, or if they would do it for me".

Tough Question. Maybe too tough to take in all at once. Step back, not to take a pass of the question, but to recognize that we are looking at this beautiful and precious thing under very bright lights and at intense magnification. To Jamie's family's way of thinking, this answer might be just the empirical evidence they understand. But for the rest of us, we are more comfortable with some 'poetic patina' lightly spread across our focus.

Besides, how would we ever truly know if we would take a bullet for each other until it was too late? While that is not the point of love, that old preacher's question does point to the depth and power of love. People have felt this emotion to the extent that they were willing to lay down their life for another. Do you?

With such power, you would expect that love takes very little thought or effort on your part. Those with much experience with love know that the opposite is true. Sure, love is patient and kind, it isn't insistent and all the rest. As such, even as precious as it is, it becomes easy to overlook and take for granted. Maybe we think that it is too good to be true or that we don't deserve it and old fears creep back in. Maybe we don't trust our instincts and think that something better is out there. Maybe we are still so caught up in our own lives that we fail to give it the attention it deserves.

This is more of that love-being-hard-work stuff. It requires you to put aside the fears and doubts. You have to look beyond yourself. It needs you to think about and work to meet the needs of the other person, often before your own needs.

For your relationship to be sustainable, love must be mutual. Each of you puts the same in and receives more in return. It grows and really does become bigger than the both of you. I suppose we could go so far as to say that love is a perpetual motion machine, pumping out more energy than it uses.

But again, once you get it up and running, you can't just sit back and take it for granted. It requires attention and intention. While this may be easy when you are at the top of your game and feeling free, love needs to be first when you are sick and tired too.

One of my counseling exercises is to ask a couple to imagine that one of them has just come back from a long and exhausting business trip with the onset of a miserable cold. The other has had a rotten day at work. They both arrive home at the same time and find that the cat has vomited on the new rug you spent too much money on. Discuss.

Love means cleaning up cat vomit. It also means working together, especially when you don't feel up to it. It means giving and receiving space. It means picking and choosing when and where you are going to call each other out on things.

Wedding vows include a vow to love the other. When we unpack what that means, we can see that it includes all of what you have just read. We vow to love at all times, good or bad. We vow to love and trust the other with the truest image of ourselves. We vow to know and to be known by each other with stark honesty and access to the deepest parts of our being.

When we love and are loved, we have the chance to become better, to grow and to move beyond our own limits and fears.

As you think about what it means to vow to love, it is helpful to look at the various forms love takes in a marriage.

Making physical love is joyous, passionate and intense. In it, two become one, as the Bible puts it. Poets and musicians the world over since the beginning of time have all come up short when they try to describe it. Fueled by hormones and a deep desire to connect and touch on such a sublime level, it is as close as we will ever get to another. So much so that it can almost become a question of where do I end and you begin?

For such a beautiful expression of love, caring and trust it can be such a confusing and confounding topic. That is because there is a world of difference between making love and just having sex.

Sex, simply on a physical level, without emotion or love is very different than it is when love is involved.

At best it is a hedonistic adventure. At worst, it is about asserting power. It is using someone, sometimes mutually, to satisfy your own wants and desires.

While it is not always about power, it is always lurking in the background. And for our purposes here, we will assume that power is involved. Because, with power, imbalance can creep in and quickly turn abusive.

But, even on a balanced, hedonistic level, it is a heady, intoxicating mix of pleasure and hormones that can kidnap you from your higher self, leaving you to chase an increasingly aloof addiction. I compare it to an addiction because it satisfies in the moment, but afterwards it leaves you less fulfilled than you were before.

Love filled sex is heady and intoxicating too, but it is much, much more. It is trusting another so deeply that you surrender yourself in the moment. It touches on the most intimate, deepest and closely held aspects of ourselves. In this sense, making love is itself merely a metaphor for this ultimate connection shared by two people.

Maybe it is in seeking to maintain this difference that is the reason for most if not all cultures' admonitions against casual sex. When you are in love, making love is just that: making, sharing, connecting with love. More, it is all of the things love is. Having sex can trample on and confuse this delicate connection. Power has a way of doing that to love. Making love and having sex are poles apart.

Not so long ago, making love was seen as the act of consummating the marriage bond. In it, two become one. Marriages without the benefit of intimate carnal knowledge could be annulled as if they never happened.

At the same time, sex outside of marriage was seen as dirty and shameful. It still is in many cultures. Most societies feel that they need to keep some level of control on sex. With power and desire at a fever pitch, the potential for abuse is strong. Rightly so, rape and incest are horribly wrong, illegal and taboo.

And yet most societies give either little or no guidance or very conflicting signals when it comes to sex. Most describe it as degrading, at least for women. Men get more of a wink and a nod. There is a huge double standard of judgement passed on sexually active men and women. Call me an optimist, but I believe that eventually all double standards fall. While we are not there yet, sex is generally seen in a more natural light. At the very least, we need to be able to have more of a dialogue about it rather than just dismissing it out of hand.

Wow, did a minister just say that? Let's be clear. I am not suggesting an 'anything goes' attitude. Sex without love is still primarily about power. As with any power issues, safeguards, laws and mores need to be firmly in place. But this is too powerful a drive to let it stay in the shadows. Clarity is much more important than sweeping it under the rug and sending conflicting social messages.

Sex infused with love seals a very powerful bond. Once you cross that boundary, I don't think you can go back to a more casual relationship. So, if this is where you think your relationship is headed, know as much as you can that love is present before you seal it.

One last point. It can be very confusing, but as much as you can, try not to confuse physical love with love. It is confusing because it is a both-and type of thing. Put another way, don't marry just for great sex.

Eventually you need to come up for air. When you do, you find that love has other levels. We have already touched on the emotional side of love. It is a yearning and longing for each other. It is a perpetual smile. It is what those around you pick up on as 'different' about you when they ask how your date went. The first time I met my wife I knew something was up. I realized that I had not laughed so freely and fully with another person in a very long time. There was an emotional connection that felt great and made me feel even greater about myself. Emotional love is another heady, intoxicating mix. Years later it is still one of the greatest driving forces in my life.

Subtler, perhaps, but equally important is mental love. I love how we think and how we connect intellectually. You trust each other with your hopes and dreams. You find that they add to and enable you to come closer to reaching those dreams.

You add to each other's collective knowledge. Thoughts and ideas seem to spark when you are together. Mental love can be another exhilarating rush. "I sent you an article on that topic we were talking about in the car the other day. Let me know what you think." You spar with each other, sharpening and honing your minds. "I have to challenge you on that. I don't think that is right at all."

Of course it is always a good idea to know when you are sparing. The goal here also is not about winning at all costs. Mental love is about each of you becoming sharper. Don't just argue by shouting differing viewpoints louder and louder until the other submits or storms off. You may become way too familiar with the phrase "winning the battle but losing the war." Rather, ask each other, "What in your past leads you to believe..." And as an added bonus, it is generally not a good idea to tack on "such a stupid, pig-headed idea."

No, really get to know why this difference is here. Have they experienced something that you haven't? You value them in so many other areas, mental love is the same. It is another foundational element. You become a better person because of this love. You don't just become smarter, you become wiser.

Most sublime is that aspect of love that reaches into your very soul. The term 'soul mate' carries real power. Your connection is so deep and obvious; it is as if you have been lovers since the beginning of time. Thinking about them becomes second nature. Your intuition grows stronger. You know when there is a disturbance in them. "I can no more imagine life without her as I can imagine life without the left side of my body.", was how one groom put it.

We live within these different aspects of love. Sometimes we get stuck in one or neglect another and a gentle nudge is needed. Your vow to love covers all of these and of course so much more. There is always something to explore. Recognizing these different elements gives you fresh ground to work on and keeps your relationship from becoming complacent and stale.

This can be more of that hard work we talked about earlier. Often we just want our spouse to give us what we want when we want it, how we want it. Right now! When you take a step back, often after you have had a door slammed in your face and you are left alone to consider things, you can identify this as immaturity. The every-day stresses and strains of life sap us of any energy to focus on our relationship. Again, this is where some of this talking-about-us skill can come in handy. Helping to overcome these times is yet another good reason for getting comfortable with talking.

But sometimes even talking isn't enough. You both are talking and talking and nothing seems to help. What gives? No matter what you do, nothing seems to help. Your partner just doesn't seem to respond to your love. They may even question your commitment to the relationship. Your feelings are just as strong. Maybe it is their commitment that should be questioned! Doubts and fears begin to raise their ugly heads. Where did things go wrong and can we fix us?

Just as love has a variety of aspects, it also has different expressions. The problem isn't your love. Rather it is the language you are using. You two are using different languages to express your love.

Dr. Gary Chapman has written one of, if not the best books on the languages of relationships and love. *The 5 Languages of Love* written in 1992 and updated often is a New York Times Bestseller. Millions of couples have used it to improve their marriages. Dr. Chapman starts out by asking the question, "What happens to love after the marriage?" The question isn't his own. He was asked it countless times by couples he was counseling.

With their honeymoon bags barely unpacked, they found that all the planning and activity leading up to the wedding was gone. In its place was an uneasiness that something wasn't quite right. What had changed? God forbid, had their love left them?

In counseling his couples, Dr. Chapman found that their love was still very much there. That wasn't the issue. I have found the same thing in my own counseling practice. Love itself isn't the issue. Rather it is how you express your love that is the cause for many marriages to fail.

Up until now, you have gone through the twitter-pated stage. You asked yourself those hard questions and realized that you were right for each other. You told everyone you were getting married and then got caught up in the whirlwind of your wedding.

Now that the hoopla has died down, you are at the point of getting on with your life together. Your perspective and horizon have expanded. Your feelings haven't changed. What has changed is their context in your life. Now you are in it for the long run. Some of those other levels of love are starting to vie for attention. What once might have been easy to overlook before now is cause for concern.

"I don't feel loved." "All the specialness of the engagement and wedding has died away." "How do I know that they still care if I can't feel it?" For their part, your spouse may well be feeling the same thing.

Trust me, this is a perfectly normal experience. Again, it isn't that love has gone. It is just as real as ever. The issue is that how the two of you express and receive love is different. And this difference didn't become readily apparent until now that things have died down.

Remember that spoiler alert before about how you two were raised with different values and ethics? Remember the old saying about how opposites attract? The same is true for how you demonstrate and show love. Dr. Chapman describes this very well by saying that you two are speaking two different love languages.

You love each other. Doesn't it make sense that you express this love in a way that your partner can feel? Before it gets too far along, I would encourage you to read his book. In the meantime, and as you are preparing to speak your wedding vows, here is a brief summary of his work as I have used it in my counseling.

We all learn how to love from how others loved us. For most of us that is from your parents and family. It also comes from how we observe others who we think are in love. Maybe you knew that your Mom and Dad loved each other because they held hands. For others it was because your Dad always brought you a souvenir when he went on a business trip. Mom made time for me when I needed to talk. Each of us learns to express love in one way or another. If we don't learn it within our families, we learn it from the people around us.

So far, so good. But what happens when you fall in love with someone who experienced love in a different way? Her mom always packed a little note in her school lunch. Your dad sat by your bedside and rubbed your back when you were sick. Now she sends you texts for no reason that seem pointless and seems unmoved when you want to hold hands.

You have each learned one way to express love. But in learning one primary way, you have wrongly assumed that it is the only way. Worse, you have assumed that your way was the right way. If I understand this as love, then surely so will my spouse. If they don't, I will just do it louder until they understand. I am going to keep sending you sweet nothing texts more and more until you finally send me one and then I will know that you love me as much as I love you. Don't make me start texting in ALL CAPS!

The good news is that you can easily discover what is the primary way your lover sends and receives love. Coming back to language, you communicate most clearly when you are both speaking the same language. Now, those emoticon filled texts are no longer interruptions at work. They are the love of the woman who loves you.

Dr. Chapman identifies the five love languages as:

1. **Words of Affirmation** This is the language of love that actually uses language. I express love by saying or writing it. A little note written in a greeting cards can be more precious than gold.
2. **Quality Time** You won't go wrong when you take the time to focus on the person who speaks this language. Listen to them, give them your attention. It will mean the world to them.
3. **Receiving Gifts** Here it is often the thought that really does count. Knowing that you remembered they loved butterflies and brought them some butterfly

ear rings will mean far more than their modest price tag.

4. **Acts of Service** What can you do to make their life a little easier? This is the question to ask when you want to speak this language of love. Again, often it is the little things that will matter the most.
5. **Physical Touch** Casual touch between two lovers can be anything but casual. In a simple touch, a gentle caress or even quick hug, love is powerfully conveyed.

From these phrases you can begin to get an idea of the different ways people experience love. If you think this is an issue for you two, by all means, get the book. He does a great job of explaining all of them.

What is your primary language? Can you spot your partner's? Learning their language lessens your frustrations, your miscommunications and fears. Talk it through. Don't assume - ask. The more you share, the easier it gets. Both of you will get very good at speaking the love language of the other. It just takes time and practice. The more fluent you become, the easier it gets.

In my experience, knowing how to express your love in the primary way your lover experiences love is the single greatest predictor of a successful marriage!

As you think about your wedding vows, do you have a clearer picture of the vow to love? There are the aspects of love: physical, emotional, mental and spiritual. There are expressions of these too. I am sometimes asked, how can someone vow to love another person? Isn't it just there? I love them until I don't anymore. I don't know if and or when that might change.

I still stand by my understanding of love as a force or power. In some ways it is from the outside of a relationship just like one of cupid's arrows. But once given, I don't think that it just stops being there. Love is a gift that requires attention and intention. Its aspects grow and change over time. How we express love also varies. When we vow to love, we are vowing to work at our love. As with most things, it is easier to work on it in a positive and proactive way while things are good. If you wait until you are reacting to problems, it can be much harder and more drastic.

Are you ready to try to put some of your own words to this crazy little thing called love? I have given you a simple framework for some of the aspects of love. What words come to mind when you think about these levels: physical, emotional, mental, spiritual? Do you know the love language you and your partner speak? I can't think of a better time to speak their language than in your vows to them.

Once you have worked through this vow writing worksheet, come back and move onto the next chapter. Far be it from me to suggest that The Beatles aren't right, that "All you need is love." But there is much more to a marriage. Marriage is a partnership in which you combine finances, careers, hopes, aspirations and dreams. We will turn our attention next to how and why we will vow to support our livelihood and what we bring to the partnership.

Vow Writing Exercise #2

1. What aspects or qualities do you deeply love about your partner?

   ____

   ____

   ____

2. What other words describe love?

   ____

   ____

   ____

3. What does loving through tough times mean to you?

   ____

   ____

   ____

4. How will you express your love for each other in a way that you will both understand?

   ____

   ____

   ____

Chapter 4

A Pledge To Support

"In plenty and in want, for richer, for poorer"

"When did you know it was love?" This is one of my icebreakers for first meetings with couples. More and more, the answer that I hear is something like, "Honestly?, when we opened a joint checking account." Who says romance is dead?

There is a good chance that one of you is saying, "Oh man, this is the boring stuff. Money, finance, budgets. Bleeech!" There is also a pretty good chance that the other of you is saying, "All right, now we are getting to the meat and potatoes of living together. Preach it, Reverend!" Most often, we get caught up in the romance and gloss over the partnership aspect of marriage. That would be fine were it not for the fact that so often it is the financials that trip up the relationship. Money causes the most fights in marriages. But, as you will soon see, it isn't money, but something deeper that is the real cause.

If the landscape of marriage has changed in recent years, that change is small compared to the change in how we make our way in the world today. It wasn't all that long ago that parents passed on their business to their children. Farms, trades, businesses were passed along from one generation to the next. The vast majority of people worked at their parent's trade.

Back then, marriage wasn't about love nearly as much as it was about business. It kept life humming along. Marriage was a way to strengthen financial relationships between families. We don't have to go back as far as European blue bloods. Wedding the daughter of the wealthiest farmer and the son of the local mill owner might not be a match made in heaven as much as a match made on Wall Street. Love had less to do with marriage than financial gain for both families involved.

It may not be as clear as these historic examples of marrying for political or financial power, but even today we see the money motivation in marriages. Going back just a generation or two, one of the benefits of marriage was a division of labor. Roles within the family were more traditionally defined. One was the 'bread-winner' bringing in the income, be it through harvest or paycheck. The other managed the home.

Today the partnership of marriage is not so much about division as multiplication.

In almost every marriage I know, both partners work to financially support the family. But with two bread-winners, confusion comes in about who is managing the home. How are roles and job responsibilities within the home being handled? Clarity is needed, assumptions must be avoided.

Beyond household chores is the much more important question of how do we make financial decisions. Sure, more money may be coming in, but where is it going? How are decisions being made? What are the goals and how do we know if we are reaching our hopes and dreams or just spinning our wheels?

Love and money may feel like diametric opposites. "Surely, you don't think that we should include the procedural processes that we will go through in making large capital decisions in our wedding vows?" Probably not, but again, it is very important to set a clear understanding of how you will set goals and make decisions. It does not have to be an either-or question of love or money. It is important that you don't lose sight of the importance of having a good financial foundation in addition to a strong emotional connection.

Trouble is, while most couples recognize the need for tending and nurturing their love, precious few see the importance of talking finances. Many never discuss it until it gets to a crisis point.

It was a perfect fall Saturday. I arrived at the wedding venue to find the groom and his guys sitting around the groom's room playing video games. Losing horribly, the groom tossed his controller to his best man, got up and came over to me. "You got a minute?'

"Sure, what's up, Bill?" "Oh, I am just enjoying the last few minutes of my childhood."

This struck me a little odd, because this thirtysomething year old groom who was a successful lawyer seemed anything but childish to me. I think I responded with something about playing video games and being married not being mutually exclusive.

"Nah, I could care less about games. What I mean is that after I am married I have more than just myself to worry about. Now I have to be a grown up."

"What do you think will be different," I asked. His response, "Before I could do what I wanted without worrying about being responsible. I had freedom, not that I ever used it. But I could have. Now I have to be serious."

I thought I knew where this was coming from. His father was a serious, no-nonsense kind of guy. I think Bill thought that marriage would steal his youth from him and replace it with his father's dour demeanor.

You may have already experienced the reality check that can come with getting married. Many couples express to me the sense that now they have to get serious about their lives. Livelihood, budgeting and career decisions certainly fit into this. It isn't just about me anymore. I have someone who depends on me. The next time life 'gets real' is if and when you decide to have children.

"I don't know.", I said. "Marriage is a big step to be sure, but my guess is that you will make it through the transition without too many regrets. You are pretty responsible. But don't give up your spontaneity. That is one of the things Jill always compliments you on. I think the change you are anticipating is just about planning for and managing decisions together."

Once you get comfortable with setting financial goals and then understanding how you hope to reach these goals, it is actually pretty freeing. Talking finances with your life partner may seem scary at first. Often we think that either the goals will be unrealistic and out of reach, or that setting a budget will mean we can never have any fun. Neither of these has to be true.

I hope that you two have found professions and jobs that provide both adequate financial and career benefits. Once that is in place, it is important to begin to plan how you will use these benefits. Having a conversation about economic dreams and goals is the first step.

- Financially, what do you want to shoot for?
- What does financial independence look like to you two?
- How much money do you need in the bank to feel secure?
- What standard of living fits for you?
- What will you do for vacations?
- How long do you want to work at your job?
- What will you live on in your retirement?

The answers to these questions will begin to bring your goals and dreams into focus.

For most people, the next step is to take stock of where you are now. Are you living beyond your means? Do you have debts that need to be addressed? The vast majority of couples I know have significant debts on which they are paying some hefty interest charges each month. Some are practically drowning in a sea of debt. Beginning to get a handle of paying these off may seem an impossible dream, but there are solutions that make debt freedom real.

A big step toward financial stability is getting in the habit of managing your money. How much do you both bring into the household? What are your necessary expenses for the basics like food, housing, and transportation? What do we need to save for in the future? Now your budget begins to come into view.

Just by reading these last few paragraphs, you are further ahead in this process than many of your friends. Recognizing the need is the first step. But now, how do we go about actually doing this without it becoming a huge fight?

While there are many people who can help you pull these together, I have found that Dave Ramsey is one of the best. In his Financial Peace University, he offers a very simple set of 'baby steps' to walk you through this process. He makes it fun and enjoyable. It is easy to stick to and see the progress. In an amazingly fast time the volatile issue of money can be defused

Beyond finances is the larger issue of career. How will your careers mesh together? Chances are that careers played into your decision to get married. When they coordinate it is a beautiful thing. When they clash, not so much.

Several years from now, one of you is in a position to accept a job promotion and advance their career. It would mean moving. What criteria factor into your decision? Is one of you more connected to your current job? What are the chances of landing a similar job in the new location? Does one career make more demands than the other? What are the long term potential benefits for both of you?

Money and earning power are some of these benefits, but job passion and satisfaction also factor in here.

These are just some of the questions to consider if you are vowing to be partners in life. Talk about your expectations with each other. The more you do, the better prepared you will be when the time comes. Again, I am not sure that I have ever heard anything about careers in wedding vows. I did hear a bride express gratitude in her vows for her husband's willingness to trek across the country with her as she pursued her career. So, while it might not have an obvious place in your vow writing, it is a very important thing to talk over, the sooner the better.

When it comes to splitting up household responsibilities, I have heard those included in more than one set of wedding vows. Just as having two bread winners multiplies the finances that support the household, it is also good to realize that you can also support each other and multiply the number of people who are tackling the household chores.

In this day and age, sharing household chores may not be as heretical as it once was. A number of years ago I came close to getting run out of a church because I let slip in a sermon that I did my own laundry and ironing and that my wife knew her way around a snow blower.

Everyone has chores they like and chores they hate. That is usually a great starting point for the discussion. Beyond that are the chores you don't mind, but don't want to get stuck doing all the time. Those, along with the chores that you both can't stand need to be divided up fairly.

Finally, it is vital to work together to make each other's' chores easier. If your spouse does the laundry, get your socks in the hamper. Not near, not in the general vicinity, definitely not hidden under the bed, but in the hamper. And no, while it hasn't happened yet, I do expect to hear socks and a hamper in someone's vows. Marriages may not fail because someone can't put their dishes in the sink, but they can fail because expectations go unvoiced. Talk. Agree. Follow through.

But wait, wasn't there something in the traditional wedding vows about obey? One of my silly jokes was to say that I auctioned the obey line off to the highest bidder and would include it in their spouse's vows. Time was, you vowed to love, honor and obey each other. Even with couples who are using traditional vows, I have not been asked to include 'obey'. Obey implies a blind following of the more powerful partner. Questions and suggestions are not welcome. Way back when, the more liberal of thinkers held that as long as love and honor were a part of the relationship, then obedience was appropriate to include in vows. If you are a part of a culture that recognizes one spouse as primary to the other, you may want to consider a mutual pledge to obey. But if you do, I hope that it will be directly related to loving and honor each other, too.

What I do hear and often see included in vows is a promise to support each other. I see support as speaking of a more equal relationship. In the areas in which we agree that you have primary responsibility, I will support you and work under your direction. Likewise, I will expect your support in those areas that I am primarily responsible for. Support is a direct response to the love and honor expressed by the other.

In a similar vein, if you have searched for traditional wedding vows, you may have come across this archaic phrase: "I doth plight thee mine troth." What on earth? I am not sure what that means, but isn't a troth something you feed a pig from?

I don't know if there is a connection with pigs, but the ancient meaning of troth was 'truth'. It is to be loyal, faithful and true.

Plight, the other unfamiliar word, means to pledge or give. Ok, that makes more sense, I am pledging to be loyal, faithful and true to you. Most of the time we think of this in the physical sense of not having sex with another person. Even more than a physical faithfulness, it has also come to carry an emotional loyalty as well. You are my closest companion and no one is going to come between us.

In the context of livelihood, I think this is a pledge of faithfulness to the partnership as well. I am giving all that I have, the sum total of what I hold dear and true, my abilities and talents, my resources and means to us. In a very real sense this is all about 'putting your money where your mouth is.'

It all follows, if I am going to be loyal and faithful to you physically and emotionally, I am also going to be faithful to our partnership financially and industriously. I will abide by and support the decisions we make, as well as the process to agree on make them. I am 'all in' in my support of us.

If you are opting for a very traditional and religious style of wedding, there is a chance that your service will include the words 'plight' and 'troth'. In a slightly less formal style, vowing to be faithful and true speaks to the same.

What once was a life run as a sole proprietorship is now a partnership. This is the deeper issue that underlies all those money fights. We fight when one or the other pulls out and tries to go it alone. I have heard plenty of spouses say that it is easier to ask forgiveness than permission when it came to a purchase. But ask yourself, is that boat more important than your marriage? Wouldn't it be better to make a mutual decision and then mutually enjoy it? Be 'all in' in your partnership.

Within your vows, how will you pledge your support and promise your commitment to your shared household? In the traditional vows, you would spell it out with words like, 'in plenty and in want', and 'for richer or poorer'. In personalized vows, you might include words like support, encourage, and 'work to bring out the best in you.'

Vow Writing Exercise #3

1. How will you work together to create a household?

   ____

   ____

   ____

2. How will you encourage each other?

____

____

____

3. What issues will you challenge each other to overcome?

____

____

____

Great news. You are more than half way through the vow writing process. As long as your wedding isn't in the next week, this might be a good time to take a quick break. Stop and look back over the changes your relationship has gone through in this process. Are you closer? I am betting that you are. I hope, too, that these conversations are getting smoother and easier to have. When you are ready, move on to the next chapter. This is good stuff, and you two are doing great work.

Chapter 5

A Pledge To Stick Together

"In sickness and in health, as long as you both shall live"

How long do you want to be married? The rest of your life? I think that is a great and reachable goal. Don't let the divorce rate scare you. There are plenty of couples who stay married their whole lives. Remember your grandmother sitting in the church in the first chapter?

Love lasts. In this chapter we look at the longevity and legacy aspects of marriage. It may feel like I am asking you to do too much, but I want you to consider that your marriage is more than just the length of time that the two of you spend together. It starts way back even before you were born with your own family. It can extend long after your time on earth has passed.

"I believe Lawrence could benefit from your wise counsel." His mother, Gwen, said in her New England boarding school accent as she was leaving church one Sunday. She was the only one who called him Lawrence. I knew him as Larry, but for the formal church wedding I had officiated a few months ago, he had acquiesced to his mother's wishes and we used Lawrence. It brought a mischievous smile to the lips of his stunning bride from Italy, Maria. "Laaawwwrrence," she said, drawing out the first part and accenting the last 'e'.

"I will be happy to give him a call. Any particular reason why?" "Let's just say that I think he could use some wisdom and guidance on settling into his new marriage," she replied through her slightly clenched teeth.

When I called, he sighed and I could sense that he wished that his mother would mind her own business for once. We agreed to meet for coffee. When I saw him I could tell that it was a good thing that his mother had intervened. Normally confident and upbeat, Larry looked down and would not maintain eye contact. When I asked how married life was going, he replied in a whisper, "She threw a pot of spaghetti."

"At you?"

"No, at the wall, but it was pretty close to me."

"What happened."

"She was having trouble figuring out how much lemon concentrate was the equivalent to the juice of one lemon to add to the salad dressing. All I did was offer to call mother. The next thing I know, the pot is flying, my kakis are stained and she had stormed out. In retrospect, I probably should have looked up the conversion rate myself instead of bringing mother into the mix. Maria is having a hard time connecting with her. They are so very different. I feel like I am in some sort of romantic comedy. You know my family. We are very old school. Mother is so uptight. Father is very regimented. 'Everything in its place and a place for everything' and all that. Maria is so, so spontaneous and alive. I love that about her, or at least I did."

Larry looked up from his coffee and went on. "Don't get me wrong. I love my parents and I know that they love me. It is just that we are much more reserved about showing emotion. I remember seeing a couple kiss on TV when I was little and being fascinated by it. Mother said that it was what some people did when they were insecure and needed to be reassured."

Wow, what a contrast! I knew that Larry's family was reserved and that Maria was, well, anything but reserved. "Sounds like some things are getting lost in translation. Most of the time, we learn how to live with another person from watching our own families operate. Sure, we see other families, but our own is the deepest, the one we fall back on for guidance."

"Yeah, I get that. I knew that we were very different, that our families and upbringing were poles apart. That was – is - a big part of Maria's allure. I want to break out and be more spontaneous. My problem is how do I trust her?"

"To not throw another pot of spaghetti?" I asked.

"Not that. Truth be told, I kind of liked it," Larry said with a sheepish grin. "No, the real confusing part came later. After she came back, she went about as if nothing had happened. I walked on eggshells for the rest of the weekend. I didn't want to revisit it, but I think that I need to. Part of me thinks that emotional explosions are just part of who she is."

"And the other part...?" I trailed off..

"Thinks she's crazy!" he said with a laugh. "No, she isn't crazy. It's just that, outside of that romantic comedy, I don't have a frame of reference.

We went on to talk about the differences between the two family cultures. In time, Larry broached the subject with Maria. She surprised him by saying that she was having trouble knowing where he was with their relationship. She confessed to feeling as if she was walking on eggshells. The two of them came to see me several times to talk through these things. When they were both able to step back and look at things with a fresh perspective, they were able to see that their love was certainly much stronger than their cultural differences. When they left one session, Maria stiffly shook my hand and then Larry grabbed me in a bear hug and kissed both my cheeks.

As we turn now to look at the third area of marriage and vows, longevity, we need to first look back on from where you both came.

There are all sorts of cultures and subcultures. We all have them and hardly any of us think that ours stinks. Chances are, you learned how to be in a marriage by watching how your elders interact. Some are on one end of the continuum, formal and stiff. Clarity of thought and reason rule the day. Affection and emotion are reserved for behind closed doors. On the other end of the spectrum, life is lived to the hilt, full of gusto and spice. Spontaneity and freedom lead to passion and emotion.

I find that the old saying 'opposites attract' is especially true here. While I think that it can also be healthy for a relationship, as with most everything else, communication is key.

One of the earliest bits of relationship wisdom came from my dad. It was one of the few times in my childhood that I remember there being a cold chill in the air between my parents. My dad looked up at me over the newspaper he was reading and from out of nowhere said, "Robbie, it all comes down to communication." My mother "humphed" in the other room as her way of saying, 'You sure got that right, buster!'

Understanding where you have each come from is as important as understanding how you each express your individual languages of love and affection. It isn't about right or wrong. It is about communicating in ways that you each understand.

There is much more to what you each learned from your own families. Chances are great that you will need to be clear about the expectations each family has about how they will interact with your new family.

Whose family will you spend which holidays with?

What are the boundaries when it comes to what gets shared? You may have already seen that each family has expectations and even demands for your time and attention. I often see this at weddings. Setting and maintaining clear boundaries around your own families may not rise to vow level, but it is very important. And if it seems challenging now, it will likely become even harder as you go along. This is especially true if and when you start having children.

Your vows are the foundation upon which you build your legacy. In general, the stronger the foundation, the brighter the future. If that future legacy includes children, how you intend to raise them needs to be unified and clear.

Do you want children? Can you have your own? Will you adopt? How will you share the parenting responsibilities? How many children will you have? When will you begin? I realize that these questions may sound premature. At this point all you might need is a general understanding.

For me, I thought that my life would change when I got married. In many ways it did. But those changes were nothing compared to the changes that happened once we had children. We had talked about some of the changes beforehand. But most of the changes caught us totally off guard.

If you have gotten this far in the book, it is safe to say that you are pretty committed to your marriage. When you have children, that level of commitment needs to be at least ten times this much.

Before children, the worst case scenario is that things don't work out for the marriage. You are two mature adults. As painful as it would be, you will move on, hopefully having learned and grown from the experience. But when you add a small, dependent child into the mix, the stakes get raised big time.

Parenthood is a huge responsibility. Please do not take it lightly. Please do not think that having a child together will somehow magically fix all the issues in you and your relationship. I see parenthood as a multiplier. It multiplies and increases the things that are good about your relationship. In the same way it multiplies all the issues that are challenges for the two of you. If they are small now, they will become much bigger.

That said, having children together really does take your relationship to an entirely new level. It has been said in many ways, but my daughter in law said it best after the birth of their first daughter, "Love is watching your heart grow and exist outside your body." In the same way that the two of you have worked together to dedicate yourselves to nurturing and growing your love in your relationship, dedicate yourselves to planning, nurturing and growing the love that is your child.

Perhaps one or both of you already have children. In some way, your vows to each other extend to your children too. Being a step parent is no easy task. Not only can your own parents and families put pressure on your relationship, but your children do too. It is crucial that the two of you understand where your boundaries are when it comes to being parent and step parent. In case you havenít already figured it out, the marriage stuff takes a lot of talking and reaching agreement!

When one or both partners have children and the children are old enough to understand, I like to include them in the wedding ceremony. They are entering a new family. As such, they need to respect it and abide by it. It is equally important for your children to hear that you two will be loving parents who welcome them into your new family.

Time was, if you raised your children to a similar level that your parents raised you, they would go off on their own and have a better quality of living. It was the American Dream to see your children surpass you. It just seemed to happen naturally. When we look back at the past decade or so, we can see that the American Dream no longer happens just on its own. It takes hard work and determination to lift your children above where you were when you struck out on your own.

This is the longer view of what I mean by the term 'legacy.' My financial planner says that he gets some pretty confused looks when he challenges and encourages his clients to think about not just having enough money to live on in their retirement, but also in creating a lasting legacy for their children.

The first time he asked me this question, my first thought was, I don't want to raise entitled, silver-spooned children! I love my kids, but really, they need to make it on their own. If they think they are just going to live off of some trust fund, then I have done them a disservice. I can look back now at this thought and see that it assumes I have done nothing to instill in them the sense of responsibility and caring for whatever legacy I pass on to them. As they have grown and matured, I see that assumption is wrong. They do have a strong sense of responsibility and desire to thrive. It isn't about just getting by, sponging off the family. Rather, it is about building on and adding to what has come before.

What legacy will your marriage leave? If children are involved, some of that legacy will be flesh and blood.

How you raise your children is much more important than what you pass on to them. If children are not in your future, your legacy extends to the larger community. What cause would you like to advance?

Legacy also means the mark you make in your lives together. Will those around you know more about what commitment means by watching you? Will you add to the meaning of love, trust and dependability?

Okay, we have looked backward in time from where you have come. We have peeked into the future to the next generation as well as the legacy you will leave. Looking forward comes with a basic assumption. That assumption is that you two are in this for the long run. It's a good assumption. But the road to divorce court is paved with this assumption. Put another way, "love is grand. Divorce is ten grand."

What does it mean to be in this for the long run? In the next chapter you will meet a couple who gave me some good ideas about longevity. In the meantime, though, what is your experience? If your parents are still married, why? If they aren't, what can you learn from their experience? How about other couples? Who do you know who has been married twenty years? Fifty years? They might be a good couple to sit down with and ask them for their advice and pointers. Learn from them.

Every couple I know who have a long term relationship point to communication as the biggest key. And sooner, rather than later. A surgeon friend puts it this way, "I operate on the living, not the dead." Work through the issues that come between you while they are fresh and small. Letting them grow and avoiding them allows them to become familiar, comfortable and expected. You can look around at other couples who have let this happen and rationalize that everyone puts up with it.

Or worse, your commitment can begin to slip and slide away. You end up just going through the motions until you don't anymore. While the grass may look greener on the other side, most everyone will tell you divorce is hell.

Back in the 60s and 70s there was a brief movement that sought to change the wording from "as long as you both shall *live*" to "as long as you both shall *love*". The idea was that marrying for a lifetime was outdated. It put too much pressure on young kids to know what they were going to want in a spouse way out in the future. A friend tried to convince me of this way of thinking by saying that this lower expectation would remove divorce from our culture. Once they stop loving each other, people will just move on. No harm, no foul.

Others tried to put a time limit on their commitment. They suggested that marriage should be a contract that expired after ten years. "Who knows, by then we might want to renew for another ten." To my way of thinking I am thankful that neither of these found much traction. There is simply too much at stake to water down the level of commitment you need to bring to your marriage.

Commitment comes from within. It isn't about the other person. It is about you being willing to work with each other. It is about your word and your intention being your bond. It is putting your mind to doing what needs to be done.

Are you committed to this marriage? If religion factors into your thinking, this is where the sacredness of the vows comes into play. Say to your spouse, "I am committing to living together as husband and wife before you, our friends and family, and God."

I have not heard anyone end their vows with the familiar, 'so help me God,' but I think that also fits in here. This is a big step and it sometimes takes all the help we can find.

When you commit to something you find that you have an inner strength you probably didn't know was there. You commit to building a lasting legacy. You come to trust in and depend on each other. You share your sources of income as well as your responsibilities. Throughout your careers you add to your common household. When your careers have run their courses, you share in your retirements. This is one of the great benefits of marriage, someone to be there for you, not just now, but in all the years to come. This is the real reason why wedding vows don't come with expiration dates.

I got a call from the owner of one of the wedding event center I work with. She asked if she could have a favor. "Of course," I said. "I would like you to perform a wedding in a couple of weeks, pro bono," she said. Over the years, this woman has referred me to plenty of couples, so I was all set to say yes, but she went on.

"The groom has a brain tumor and he is terminal. They are a young couple and would really like to celebrate their wedding before he passes," she explained. "They came in looking for just a very small ceremony, but once

I heard their story I thought we need to do all that we can for these folks. Can I count on you?"

Amanda and Brian were an amazing couple. It was such a joy to work with them. Of course, there wasn't a dry eye when they got to the ending of their vows "in sickness and in health, 'til death do us part." But much more powerful was the strength and conviction that came through as they said it.

They knew the power and importance of being there for each other no matter how much time they had left. It isn't an easy conversation to have, but it is important to know that your future spouse will be there for you, come what may.

This section of the vows can be the toughest to write. It requires you to think about what your life will be far out in the future. Chances are, there will be plenty of twists and turns between here and there. Most of which you will have no idea of until you are smack dab in the middle of them. That's okay, your vows are not predictions. They are guides. They will come in very handy when you are in the middle of life.

Vow Writing Exercise #4

1. What does this commitment mean to you?

   ____

   ____

   ____

2. In what ways do you see your love growing?

____

____

____

3. What will your legacy be?

____

____

____

You have now worked through the three main sections of vows: Love, Livelihood and Longevity. Vows that include all of these are strong and solid. Remember that lovers' leap image at the beginning? Will you two fly off into the wild blue yonder? You will with vows that take these areas into account. That said, there are such things as 'dealbreakers'. I see vows as permanent, not absolute.

Chapter 6

Dealbreakers

"Forsaking all others as long as we both shall live"

Permanent? Absolute? What's the difference? Vows are serious business. They are not meant to be gotten into or out of easily. You are giving another person your word that you are going to stay married to them in good times and in bad, for the rest of your life. In many cultures, you are vowing to do this not just before them, but also before God, for eternity. That is the permanent part.

Absolute implies that there is absolutely no exception or reason why your vow can ever be broken. I do not believe that.

You are an adult of sound mind who is able to make life changing decisions for yourself. When you vow to become a married couple on your wedding day, you are making that vow based on all the information and experience you have with that other person up to that point.

If they have not been completely truthful with you, or if they do something in the future that harms you, can you be released from your vow? I believe that you can. That is what I mean by saying that vows are not absolute.

At a bare minimum, the non-absoluteness of vows should serve as some hindrance to your spouse, not to betray you. There are boundaries. If you cross one, there will be consequences.

On a bigger scale, this also means that you both actively work to maintain and improve the health of your marriage. Being clear with each other from the beginning as to what is not acceptable is vital. It isn't just about being clear. It is also important in that should either one of you find yourself drawn down a path that leads to such a violation of your vows, you recognize sooner, rather than later what that will mean.

It is not just the act that crosses the boundary. It is everything that leads up to the betrayal. Before you commit, you plan. Before you plan, you decide. Before you decide, you close off communication with your spouse. Before you close off communication, you recognize there is a problem. Before you recognize there is a problem, you are not truthful. It goes all the way back to what George Carlin used to refer to in his comedy sketch about committing sin, "Ya gotta wanna!"

Let's be very clear here. This is not about one partner driving the other to betrayal. There is no blaming the victim implied. Betrayal is a process. There are steps along the way. The sooner you address something is amiss, the better. You have both already put so much into this relationship. As much as is in your power, work together to find a way to fix things while they can still be fixed.

Guess what? It's time for another conversation with your mate. What are the dealbreakers you each have? One that is almost universal is abuse - physical, verbal, emotional or sexual. Abuse is using your power to inflict pain and damage onto another. Much has been made about abuse in recent years. Rightly so. Any form of abuse must be recognized and dealt with immediately. In my role as a clergy person, if I ever had suspicion that one spouse was abusing another, I had a moral and legal obligation to address it. If you are being abused and think that it will get better once you get married, you are sadly mistaken. Get help immediately. There are clergy, social workers, psychologists, shelters and police who can help. I won't say that an abuser isn't capable of change. I am saying that the situation will not change without professional outside help.

Fidelity is another dealbreaker that is almost universal. Being sexually faithful to your partner is a significant part of almost all cultures for good reasons.

Earlier we spoke of the difference between having sex and making love. Both are incredibly powerful human experiences. The power between hormones and emotions requires very careful handling.

Over time, that power changes. One of you may have a stronger desire for it than the other. This will ebb and flow between you. Open communication is very important here.

Some cultures hold that you can separate love from sex. If it is possible, it is well beyond the scope of this book. Should you want your relationship to deviate from physical faithfulness, I would suggest working with a professional therapist to help you both sort through the emotional, psychological and physical implications of an open relationship.

This is another dealbreaker that will not just go away on its own.

Should you or your spouse break your faithfulness, run, do not walk, to a professional marriage counselor.

How about trust? For many this is another dealbreaker. This is about being open and honest. Those are two separate things. Being open means that you do not keep secrets from each other.

Many years ago, a young church member called me very upset. He had been looking over their bank statement and noticed that his wife had made a large cash withdrawal. When he asked her about it, she became very defensive, ran and locked herself in the bathroom. She pleaded with him not to be mad and to trust her.

I asked if anything in her recent behavior was suspicions? "Not specifically, but I did see her car parked outside the liquor store last week. I didn't think anything of it, but now I am wondering if I am not wanting to see something. I don't think she has a drinking problem, but now I don't know."

I suggested that he keep an eye on things, be supportive and try not to be confrontational until he had more information. We left it that he would come by the church the next Saturday to talk.

Saturday rolled around and both Bill and Sarah came in wearing sheepish grins and birthday hats! She had been planning a surprise party for him. She replayed the whole scene from her perspective, saying that she didn't know what to do when he asked about the money. Her first response was to get defensive and then she was afraid that she was going to burst out laughing when she imagined the look on his face when everyone yelled "SURPRISE!"

This isn't the kind of openness I am talking about. But it is a good example of how important openness is in a relationship. Bill thought they had a good level of trust. He said that somewhere deep down he knew that he could trust her. Still, his mind worried about it and couldn't let it go. If that openness wasn't there to begin with, it could have been a much worse situation.

Openness is pretty hard to fake. It comes over time as you share your hopes and dreams with each other. Usually it is mutual and reciprocal. The more you share, the more your partner shares. It leads to vulnerability. As you come to trust each other, the more open you can be. It is a fragile thing. The more you learn about each other, the more pain you can inflict. Even so, without openness it is impossible for trust to grow.

It is the same thing when it comes to honesty. First and foremost, you must be honest with yourself. That can be pretty hard. We generally get pretty good at telling ourselves little lies to rationalize and float through life. But as we grow, we learn that it is better to set these aside as they do not help in the long run.

When we let someone into our inner circle of trust, they can see these lies. In a good way, they can help you get beyond your need for them. Honesty can be like a scalpel. Used with skill, compassion and a genuine desire to help, it can improve you and draw out your better and higher self. In a bad way, it can be used to slash and tear a person apart.

Or, when not used at all, a lack of honesty can lead to a co-dependency. It takes a lot of courage and love to confront your loved one with an honesty that borders on brutal. But then, isn't that why we search for a life partner? Someone who can help us become a better, deeper, richer, fuller person?

Now, sooner or later, every spouse is confronted with the conundrum known by the question, "Do these pants make my butt look big?"

Option 1: Lie, "No, not at all."
Option 2: Honesty, "Yep, they sure do."
Option 3: Brutal Honesty, "Nope, your butt was big before you put those pants on."
Option 4: Deft Deflection, "That isn't a flattering color on you."

I share this simply to highlight that while honesty is vital, it is also a good idea to know when and how much is required.

More to the point, over the years, I have been presented with various business opportunities. Being open with my wife, I have shared these and asked her opinion. I tend to not just see the glass as half full. I tend to believe that at any minute it is going to be overflowing with all sorts of magical goodness. My wife is more the realist. She asks hard questions and on more than one occasion has declared me crazy for even considering trading our cow for a handful of magic beans.

At the time, I did not like what she said. But time and time again I have seen the wisdom in her opinion. She once confessed that it was so hard for her to be honest with me that she thought about just keeping her mouth shut and letting me make what she thought was a bad decision. I am glad that she speaks her mind. We have found, again and again, that the truth lies somewhere between our two opinions. When we listen to each other we end up in a much better place.

Honesty can be exhausting. But at the end of the day, I know that we are both much better as individuals and our relationship is stronger for it.

Trust is something that doesn't just happen. It is both learned and earned.

Openness and honesty work together to create the foundation for trust. We learn to trust and to be trusted over time, with little things at first. As we learn to take each other at our word and in turn, to speak our truth, we become skilled at the art of trust.

Then, most often when we don't expect it, we find ourselves in a situation that tests our trust. When we pass these tests, we earn the right to be entrusted with deeper and more precious things. No doubt, you have earned each other's trust before you came to know that he or she was the right one. Let that continue. You may also find that this thinking comes in handy should you two find yourselves parenting. Help your children to learn how to be trustworthy. As they become trustworthy, allow them to earn more of your trust by entrusting them with more. Be careful not to go too fast and you will be amazed at how quickly their trustworthiness grows.

Okay, so faithfulness and trust are the two big dealbreakers, right? Isn't this as far down the dealbreaker path as we need to go? Not quite. There is one more and I am sorry, but it is a pretty rude dealbreaker to consider. It is what brought you two here in the first place – Love.

What happens if we fall out of love with each other? Sit down. This is important.

Many marriages do not succeed. When I have asked, most ex-couples tell me that they stopped loving each other. Oh, they may have cheated or stopped communicating, but before that came the loss of love.

Early on, love is easy. It is a bubbly, giddy, sensual, hell of a ride. But after a time, that fast, frenetic pace slows. Love stops drawing attention to itself. Somehow, we find the demands of life pressing in on us.

Several years ago, I had the opportunity to raft through the Grand Canyon. During those two weeks we rode our small rafts through some of the most exhilarating rapids in the world. But for much more of our time, the river was calm, even placid. Married love isn't so much one wild rapids ride right after the other as it is a gentle, deep, calm ride interspersed with amazing times of sheer joy.

If you have been together for more than a few months, perhaps you can see what I am getting at. If you are just sitting back waiting for the next rush of love, you may be disappointed to find that those rushes come farther and farther apart. If you are just along for the ride, then you may even find that over time the thrill is gone, replaced with drudgery and stagnation. You stop opening up and sharing becomes more and more shallow. You put less time and energy into your relationship and start looking elsewhere for validation. You rationalize and trivialize your relationship.

But, for every couple who finds themselves leaving Divorce Court in separate cars, there is a couple who has found the secret to life-lasting love. I have spent lots of time trying to learn from them. One of those couples is Frank and Mary.

"You really do fall in love, that's true." The second wedding I ever preformed was actually a renewal of vows ceremony for Frank and Mary. "FIFTY YEARS!" Frank said it over and over as we were planning the service. That and, "You really do fall in love. But if you want my opinion, folks don't fall out of love as much as they crawl out of it."

"Good Lord, Frank, you make it sound like a vat of quicksand!" Frank squeezed Mary's hand, looked at me, smiled and said, "And that is why I have been with her for FIFTY YEARS! She gets my jokes without me having to explain them."

Turning as serious as I ever knew him to be, Frank went on, "At first we were all over each other. I could tell you stories that would make all of us blush. Then the war came and I was off to it. We wrote a lot at first. But then things got hairy and surviving took on a whole new priority. Mail lines were spotty at best. Sometimes it would be weeks before it got through. And there would be Mary's letters, scented with lily of the valley. She wrote about life back home and what we were going to do when I came home. The worse war got, the more foreign her letters sounded. I didn't know what to write. Mostly I just told her how much I missed her."

"Once VJ Day came, I got my discharge papers and came back to her. Along with the rest of the country, we got caught up in making a living and a family and a this and a that. I would love to tell you it was all happily ever after, but that just wasn't so. Somewhere along the way I fell into the bottle."

"And then one night, this sweet and innocent woman sitting before you hit me upside the head with a choice. It was either her way or the highway. It was a rough time I tell you what. But we made it through. It was after that that I vowed I was going to turn things around. We started out small, taking a walk after dinner together. I bet we have walked around the world twelve times by now. Sometimes we would talk about our day, or the kids, or just life. Other times we just walked. But we always made time for us. I realized that this dear woman was the most precious part of life. I didn't deserve her. Hell, I did plenty to give her an excuse to leave me high and dry."

He pulled out a handkerchief and wiped his eyes. All of ours were pretty misty. "Love is hard work. The best stuff is always hard work. And this woman is the best of the best."

I knew right there and then that I wanted what they had. Years later I have come to know just how true his words were.

Here is the thing. We think that we haven't done any work to fall into love. So why should we have to do any work to stay in love? At least that is the way I thought of it for many years. When you think of love as something that comes from the outside like a gift from God or cupid's arrow, it becomes a matter of chance.

Sure, there is plenty about falling in love that is out of your control. But there is also plenty that has gone into making you who you are. Don't forget all the time and energy that went into getting you to the point you were when you met your love. It was all the work you put into you: education, character, occupation, attributes, connections, the list goes on and on. It is hard to see all of these because they are so close to who you are. But without them, without you being who you are, you would not be with who you are with. You would not have appealed to them, nor they to you.

Make no mistake, you did a lot of hard work on you long before you went on that first date that has led to planning your wedding.

So now you are here. Why wouldn't you think that you will still have to put in the work? Just as it is your intention to continue to improve yourself, your intention to continue to work on your relationship is vital to its health.

So then, is falling out of love a dealbreaker? If love is the foundation of your relationship, it seems to me that falling out of love is too late. The deal has already been broken. We need to look further back for the dealbreaker. That is the point when you stopped caring. You stopped intentionally putting in the time, energy and effort into the relationship. Not caring about your marriage is the real dealbreaker.

God forbid, but if you should ever find yourself in this situation, remember your vows. Reread them. Think back about why you made them. They can provide you tremendous guidance. Find your reason to care and rededicate yourself to it.

It doesn't matter how you got to this point, or if your spouse got here first. What matters is that you can turn things around. It doesn't have to be too late.

This is the real reason I have written this book. I hope that it is the reason why you are reading this. You do not want to stop caring about and for your marriage. Your wedding vows are how you say to your spouse and yourself just what you are committing to. It makes perfect sense to keep your vows close. If you use traditional words, understand what you are saying. Find a way to make those words your own. Say your words to each other. Dedicate yourself to them. Remember, they are called vows, because they are what you are vowing to do. You are swearing loyalty to one another. Your words become your bond.

Rededicate yourselves to them often. Use your vows to keep your love fresh. They are not magic words. The magic is in the intent that you put behind them. That magic is powerful and strong. Don't forget it, or take it for granted.

As your lives grow together, your understanding of the words of your vows will change. You will know more and more what you have gotten into. And that will be good.

The day Frank and Mary renewed their vows was beautiful. We stood under a big tree in their back yard, surrounded by their children, grandchildren and great grandbabies. As they held each other's hands and repeated their vows after me, you could feel the power. It was a connection with everyone there. It was a connection with the generations that passed before them and the generations that would follow, with the tree, the house, the world, even the universe. Love is the strongest power there is. In that perfect moment, we knew we were standing in the presence of the holy and that all was right with the world.

My hope and prayer for you is that someday, maybe even FIFTY YEARS from now, you will be standing under a big tree, reciting your own wedding vows. As you look into the eyes of your beloved, you will understand the true power of love. May you celebrate the joys of your lives together. May you forgive yourselves for your mistakes. And in that moment may all be right with you and your world. Close your eyes and imagine that moment. Now open your eyes and start to move toward it.

Vow Writing Exercise #5

1. What are your dealbreakers?

   ____

   ____

   ____

2. What are your partner's dealbreakers?

   ____

   ____

   ____

3. What is the positive way to state these? (for example: if lying is a dealbreaker for you, a positive word would be honesty)

____

____

____

4. How will you work with your partner to keep your vows?

____

____

____

5. How will you keep your love fresh and alive for the rest of your lives together?

____

____

____

Chapter 7

Putting It Down On Paper

Writing stuff is hard. At least I think it is. I know what I want to say, but when I go to put it on paper, it gets confusing. What should go first? How much background do I need to give so that the point I am trying to make will make sense? In what order do I put everything?

To make things worse, vows are spoken, so they need to have a flow to them. Writing vows is like writing poetry. There is an artistic aspect to how they sound, as much as a functional aspect to what they convey. I had a high school teacher who used to say that writing poetry was like putting yourself in a straightjacket and then trying to tango.

But don't worry. You have to learn to walk before you can tango. In this case, walking, or the first step is deciding what to include. During our time so far, you have gathered the raw material that will become the contents of your vows. In this chapter we will pull all of that together.

Generally the first question I get when we get to this point is "Should we write our vows together or apart?" Yes. On the one hand, it is important to have similar content. If you have both gone through the vow writing exercises, you have that part covered. Throughout the chapters, I encouraged you two to talk about these various issues. More than just a starting point for your vows, the topics for discussion in the previous chapters are the ones that will come up again and again in your marriage.

Some couples stay here and work together to create identical vows. For the couple I spoke of who created a mission statement for their marriage, working together was an important part of their process.

The only caution to this approach is to make sure that both of you are committed to the end result. There are plenty of decisions around your wedding where one partner's opinion may be more important than the other's. What colors should the centerpieces be? Which beer should the bar stock? It isn't that the other doesn't care. It is recognizing that you want the person who is more invested to be happy with the choice. This is not one of those times. You both need to be very invested in your vows. When you get to polishing and wordsmithing your vows, one of you may find it easier and take the lead. But not now, while we are still sorting out what content to include. Do not let this be a time where one of you finds yourself saying, "Whatever you want is fine with me." Both of you need to be all in if you are working together.

Other couples move on from this mutual starting point and each partner then writes their own version of their vows. Many couples I talk to say that they find a more personal element to this approach. Most couples who go this route continue it up to the ceremony. They want how they express their vows to be a surprise. Again, starting from the same place helps to insure that there isn't going to be a big disconnect between the two of you on your wedding day.

Still, you may want to ask a mutual friend to read each set of vows to make sure that they cover similar ground. Beyond the content, they can also help with harmonizing your individual styles. Your own personalities are going to come through your individual vows. I think that is a good thing. And it is also a good thing that your vows fit together in a broad way as well. In this way, your vows are coordinated and personalized at the same time.

If you are using traditional vows for your service and then sharing personalized vows privately, harmonizing the styles may not be as important. It is still good to start from the same point. Like a map, it is helpful to be looking at the same one.

Okay, I think you are ready to take your first crack at your vows. Start with your answers to the questions at the end of Chapter 2. They provide an opening that establishes your vows as uniquely written for the two of you. "From the moment I saw you waiting for me outside in the rain, I knew that our love was real…" "You won me over with your brutal honesty and infectious laugh…"

Get the idea? Remember that your goal is to personalize, not scandalize. I am sure there are plenty of little intimate details that could go in here. Keep in mind who is going to hear your vows besides your intended. This can also be the time to set the tone. Is it light and fun or formal and filled with gravity? Remember your style grid from Chapter 1. It can guide you in your word choices.

One question I often get is do we give or receive? Do I give myself to you, or do you receive me as your spouse? I have heard both, but to my way of thinking, you have given yourself by showing up for the wedding. That is, your being here is agreement enough. At the point of the vows, you are taking, or receiving your partner as their new role in your life.

The questions following Chapters 3–6 provide the meat for your vows. They can go in any order that makes sense to you. I hope that as you read those chapters and answered the questions that you had the chance to deeply think about and discuss what you are both agreeing to as husband and wife.

This is the serious part of your vows. They are set out in the three primary areas that are affected by marriage in our lives. One section may hold more importance than the others. But try to at least consider including something from each chapter.

As for the dealbreakers, you noticed that one part of the exercise was to write them as a positive as well as in their negative sense. I had you do that because "I promise to be faithful" sounds much better than "I promise not to fool around."

Dealbreakers can also be incorporated in the previous three sections. They do not need to be their own section of the vows. They may not even sound like dealbreakers, to your family and friends, but the two of you know how important they are.

Looking at all of these four chapters, this is a joining together of two people in a common purpose. At the end of the day, you are joyfully binding your hearts together as one. This is what you are agreeing to with full and loving hearts.

In addition to love, highlight the importance of livelihood and longevity in your vows. When you do this, their power and your conviction shine through. No one who hears your vows has any question that you two know what you are getting yourselves into.

Ending that last sentence with a preposition is a no-no for some. This is a good time to suggest that you think a little bit about the grammar you use in your vows. I see grammar's primary role is to help you be clear in what you are saying, not satisfying your aunt, the family grammar police.

Running your vows through a grammar checking app is a good idea. But also remember that you are going to be reading these aloud. How they sound and how easy they are to say is usually more important than a split infinitive or dangling participle.

This is when we start to put them to music and see how they dance off your tongue. At this point in the process, you may find that it is better to say your vows rather than write them. That way you can better hear their rhythm and flow. I like alliteration, stringing several strategic statements together with words that start with the same sound. I also like balance and symmetry where the sentence structures are constant. But not too constant. A change to the structure lets people know that what comes next is important.

Once you have polished your vows up a bit, it may be time to ask a friend to listen to you read them out loud. If that feels too weird, this is another time to send them to someone and ask them what they think (I bet your officiant would be willing to read them through and offer feedback.) In the end, these vows are your own. But the input of others can be very valuable. If you mutually agree, you can certainly read each other's vows beforehand. But there is something magical about hearing them for the first time in that perfect setting.

Generally, I discourage couples from memorizing their vows. It is just too emotional and too important. Allow your officiant to give you your vows either on paper or by repeating them, phrase by phrase.

At the rehearsal or on the day of the ceremony, give your vows to the person who is conducting your service. I suggest that even if you are going to memorize your vows.

I did a wedding once for a television actor and actress. When I suggested that they give me their vows for the ceremony, the groom said with a flourish "Please sir, I am an acTOR!" I was glad that I had pressed him because when we got to his vows during the ceremony, he looked deeply into his bride's eyes, paused for a beat, and then another and another and then, in a very loud stage whisper said, 'WHAT'S MY LINE?"

Two last pieces of advice. The first one is remember as you are writing your vows to actually include that you are making a vow or a promise. It may sound silly, but in the midst of everything, I have seen couples forget to say in their vows that they are actually vowing to do what they say they are going to do. Most of the time this will fit at the beginning. "I vow to take you as my wife / husband / partner..." It doesn't have to go at the beginning, just make sure that it goes somewhere in whatever language you feel fits you two.

The second bit of advice also sounds a bit silly, but I have had several couples come back afterwards and thank me for reminding them during the rehearsal to take a moment before their vows to stop and take it all in. Look into the eyes of your partner. Feel the love and joy that surrounds you two. Look out at your family and friends that have gathered with you. Remember those who aren't there in person, but there in spirit. Drink it all in so that you can remember it for years and years to come.

So, are you ready to give it a shot? It isn't as hard as I made it sound before. Use the lines here to work out your first draft.

Introduction:

____

____

____

1st section (Love, Livelihood or Longevity)

____

____

____

2nd section

____

____

____

3rd section

____

____

____

Now before you go, there is one more thing to discuss. If you remember nothing else from this book remember this.

Vows are not what you say. Vows are what you do.

Marriage occurs in the hearts of two people. Words do not touch hearts nearly as deeply as actions. You two have already become as one in an inward bond. Your wedding is the outward expression of that bond. In the same way, so are your vows. You say them in front of 'God and everybody' to recognize their importance in your life.

You are changed by your vows. Not by the words of your vows, but rather in the very act of making them. You have a new direction and purpose in life. I do not think it is making too much out of vows to say that it is this new purpose and direction, this change that allows us to say that there really is an eternal element to them. If your grandmother is sitting up close for your wedding, your grandfather having passed on, I believe that there is a bond that exists still between them. I can't explain it. It is far more complex than our simple minds can conjure, far beyond trying to make sense of who is married to who in the great beyond. I just know that the power of your vows are real. And if you have gotten this far, there is a pretty good chance that you believe that too.

So, what is left to do? Not forget your vows or allow yourselves to take them for granted. For this power, the power of love isn't loud and showy. It is quiet and unassuming. As such, it is easy to neglect and forget it. I suggest that you find ways to remind yourselves of its strength, beauty and joy each and every day.

Frame your vows and put them in a prominent place in your house. But not in some stuffy room you only go in once in a while. Put them by the door you go in and out of. Put them in your bedroom so that they are the first thing you see when you wake and the last thing you see before sleep.

Pull them off the wall and read them to each other now and again. Consult them when you are facing a challenging decision. Speak them in their loving tones. Draw on their strength for courage and hope. And then, years from now, when they are weathered and worn from the passing of time and the fullness of life, you will look at them and know that your life has been good.

May you be blessed in this joyous venture all the days of your lives together.

Chapter 8

In Case of Emergency, Break Glass

I didn't want to include this chapter since, in some ways, it goes against what I am trying to accomplish in this book. But in the end, this isn't about me. It is about you. What follows are lines from some of the vows I have heard over the years.

I have arranged them not in actual vows themselves, but rather as examples from the various sections I suggest to include. Read them over if you need a nudge to get unstuck. If you do, try to remember where you needed help. Chances are, this same issue will come up again in your lives together.

Traditional Wedding Vows

I, ___, take thee, ___, to be my wedded husband/wife, to have and to hold, from this day forward, for better, for worse, for richer, for poorer, in sickness and in health, to love and to cherish, till death do us part, according to God's holy ordinance; and thereto I pledge thee my faith [or] plight thee my troth.

Sample Introductions

I, _____, take you, _____, to be my husband/wife, from here to the moon and back...

From the moment I saw you at the coffee shop, I knew that we were meant for each other. I take you this day to be my husband/wife...

They say that love is blind, but that is not true for me. I look at you and my heart melts...

From your brutal honesty to the way you wrinkle your nose when you are reading, I love everything about you...

Sample Vows About Love

...You see the best in me. I see that best reflected in you and can't help but become better myself...

...We have seen each other through some dark times. Through it all we have become stronger. That is what love does...

...I don't know where your breath ends and mine begins. Your hand fits my hand. Your soul fits my soul...

Sample Vows About Sharing A Household

...I will follow you wherever your career takes us...

...I vow to grow with you as our family grows...

...I promise to listen and not fix...

...Our children will know the joys of 'Flapjack Fridays' and of letting 'Mommy/Daddy Sleep Saturdays'...

Sample Vows About A Lifetime Commitment

...I promise to grow with you, not old and cranky, but better and wiser...

...What we plant today, our children will water tomorrow and one day our grandchildren will play under...

...Our legacy of love goes forth this day from the union of our hearts and souls...

Dealbreakers Framed As Positives

...I will be worthy of your trust...

...With my body, mind and soul I will honor you and our love...

...I pledge myself to putting our marriage first and foremost in my life...

Sample Endings

...I make this solemn vow with love and joy in my heart.

...I commit to strengthening these bonds between us each and every day that we draw breath.

...I love you, forever and ever and ever.

FrameYourVows.Com

CONGRATULATIONS! You have worked hard to write and understand your wedding vows. These vows create a strong foundation for your marriage. The best way to remember your vows is to display them in your home. Let them be a constant reminder of your commitment and dedication. Let them inspire and encourage you to deeper levels of love and joy.

- Visit www.FrameYourVows.com
- Upload your vows
- Create your own individual work of art
- Display your vows in your home

ABOUT THE AUTHOR

The Rev. Dr. Rob Hundley grew up in Fort Worth, Texas. After graduating from the University of Texas at Austin he earned his master's degree from Andover Newton Theological School in Newton Centre, Massachusetts. Rob went on to receive a Doctorate of Ministry in Preaching from Chicago Theological Seminary. He served churches in the United Church of Christ in Connecticut and Colorado. He has conducted hundreds of weddings across the country. While Rob has moved on from local church ministry, he still performs dozens of weddings each year. Additionally, he has a career in counseling and massage therapy. "We really do carry our issues in our tissues. I seek to address the body, mind and spirit." He lives with his wife, Betsy. Together they enjoy their adult children, grandchildren and a great many pets.